*Firekeeper*

NEW & SELECTED POEMS

# Firekeeper

## Pattiann Rogers

MILKWEED EDITIONS

Published in 1994 by Milkweed Editions. Printed in the United States of America.
The text of this book is set in Centaur, with Arrighi as the italic.
97 98     5 4 3
*First Edition*

Milkweed Editions is a not-for-profit publisher. We gratefully acknowledge support
from the Elmer L. and Eleanor J. Andersen Foundation; Dain Bosworth Foundation;
Dayton Hudson Foundation for Dayton's and Target Stores; Ecolab Foundation;
General Mills Foundation; Honeywell Foundation; Jerome Foundation; John S. and
James L. Knight Foundation; The McKnight Foundation; Andrew W. Mellon
Foundation; Minnesota State Arts Board through an appropriation by the
Minnesota State Legislature; Musser Fund; Challenge and Literature Programs of
the National Endowment for the Arts; I. A. O'Shaughnessy Foundation; Piper
Family Fund of the Minneapolis Foundation; Piper Jaffray Companies, Inc.;
Ripley Memorial Fund; Rollwagen Fund of the Minneapolis Foundation; Star
Tribune/Cowles Media Foundation; Surdna Foundation; James R. Thorpe
Foundation; Unity Avenue Foundation; Lila Wallace-Reader's Digest Literary
Publishers Marketing Development Program, funded through a grant to the Council
of Literary Magazines and Presses; and generous individuals.
Library of Congress Cataloging-in-Publication Data

Rogers, Pattiann, 1940–
    Firekeeper  :    new & selected poems / Pattiann Rogers.
      p.   cm.
    ISBN 1-57131-400-8
    I. Title
    PS3568.0454F57    1994
    811'.54—dc20                              94-10655
                                                 CIP

*For the celebration,*
*and for all the celebrants,*
*every one of them, everywhere.*

## Acknowledgments

I wish to thank the editors of the following publications in which the new poems in this book first appeared.

*American Poetry Review:* Eating Death; *Cutbank:* The Need to Adore, This Kind of Grace; *Georgia Review:* Till My Teeth Rattle, Emissaries; *Gettysburg Review:* Berry Renaissance, Still Life Abroad, Creating Transfiguration, The Fancy of Free Will, For Any Known Fact: Nude Walking Alone on a Beach in Moonlight; *Hudson Review:* The All-Encompassing; *Iowa Review:* Trial and Error, The Image in a World of Flux; *Orion:* The Natural Nature of Late Night Prayers; *Paris Review:* God Alone, Life in an Expanding Universe; *Poetry:* The Laying-on of Hands; *Poetry Northwest:* Are Some Sins Hosannas?, Infanticide; *Prairie Schooner:* Apple Disciples; *TriQuarterly:* Goddamn Theology; *Western Humanities Review:* If Dying Means Becoming Pure Spirit; *Wilderness:* Another Little God, In My Time.

I wish also to thank Robert Adams and Mandy Evans for their help with specific suggestions when I was selecting poems for inclusion in this book. My loving gratitude to my family and to many friends, editors and students for their enriching conversations, correspondence and interest during the years when the poems in this volume were written.

I am extremely grateful for the generous support and encouragement given me by the Guggenheim Foundation, the National Endowment for the Arts, and the Lannan Foundation.

# CONTENTS

from **The Expectations of Light**

from **The Tattooed Lady in the Garden**

from **Legendary Performance**

New Poems
## Old Spiral of Conception

from

*The Expectations of Light*

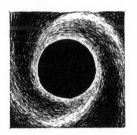

## Hiring the Man Who Builds Fires for a Living

He comes when I ask him, during the last half hour
Of evening, begins with his earthen circles,
His rings of rock. Infuriating swagger,
He carries about him the distinct odor of mitigating humus.

But he knows his business. He disappears again and again
Into the trees, taken as if the forest knew him personally,
And comes back always from another direction, his arms
Full of branches having fallen themselves
From great heights without wings nights ago.

When the trees are not totally black, not yet fully entrenched
In the grey sky, imagine how he kneels down
And bends close, how he proceeds with the arrangement.
What is it he believes about this altar? He lays
Each stick religiously as if it had grown
Toward this place from the beginning. What is he whispering
To those dried-up leaves as if they had souls?
There's a blessing here he definitely finds amusing.

I can never see at this point what it is he moves
With his hands or how he concentrates on molding
The invisible as if he could manipulate prophecy, shape
The promise to fit the gift to come. Perfect sculptor,
He knows his element thoroughly.

Watching the deep blue curtains as they fall constantly now
Among the dark trees, I admit
He knows with his breath how to make flame live.

And in the midst of it all, what can I think of a man
Who has created in this black forest tonight
A popping circus of blue-gold brilliance plummeting
With such acrobatic radiance that I laugh out loud myself?
Well, I hired him on faith. He was obliged to be
More than I expected.

## In Order to Perceive

At first you see nothing. The experience is similar
To opening your eyes wide as white marbles
Inside the deepest cave, beneath tons of limestone,
Or being awake in a dark room, your head
Under a heavy blanket.

Then someone suggests there is a single candle
Wavering far off in one corner, flickering red.
You think you see it
As someone else draws your attention to the sharp
Beaming wing tips, the white end of the beak,
The obvious three points of the wild goose overhead
And the seven-starred poinsettia to the west, the bright
Cluster at its belly.

You are able to recognize, when you are shown,
The sparks flying from the mane of the black stallion,
The lightning of his hooves as he rears,
And in the background a thick forest spreading
To the east, each leaf a distinct pinprick of light.

Then you begin to notice things for yourself,
A line of torches curving along a black valley,
A sparkling flower, no bigger than a snowflake,
Shining by itself in the northwest coordinate.
It is you who discovers the particular flash
Of each tooth inside the bear's open mouth and the miners
With their lighted helmets rising in a row.

How clear and explicit, you tell someone with confidence,
That ship, each separate gleaming line of its rigging,
The glowing dots of the oars, the radiating
Eyes of the figure on the prow, the corners
Of each sail lit.

Soon there is no hesitation to the breadth
Of your discoveries. Until one night during the long
Intensity of your observation, you look so perfectly
That you finally see yourself, off in the distance
Among the glittering hounds and hunters, beside the white
Shadows of the swans. There are points of fire
At your fingertips, a brilliance at the junctures
Of your bones. You watch yourself floating,
Your heels in their orbits, your hair spreading
Like a phosphorescent cloud, as you rise slowly,
A skeleton of glass beads, above the black desert,
Over the lanterned hillsides and on out through the hollow
Stretching directly overhead.

## For Stephen, Drawing Birds

They catch your eye early, those rising black
Out of the water oaks at dusk or those skimming
The grey lakes at dawn. You know you must learn
Them by name, calling the redstart, pointing out
The towhee, the slate-colored junco. You begin
To trace their drummings through the forest, the click
Of their matings in the rocks, and grow accustomed
To waiting, sketchbook in hand, for the mottled
Vireo to nurse at the fruit tree, the woodcock to rise
To the spring willow bait. You are patient
With the snow goose appearing at the bottom of the reeds
And the thrasher untangling itself from the hedgerow.
What luck, the day you find a whole cliff of gannets,
Their pale yellow heads as smooth as eggs, their eyelids
And nostrils distinctly blue.

Matching pencil to feather, you begin to take them
One by one—the marbled owl pulling at the skull
Of the lemming, the dusky tanager in the afternoon
Snipping at dragonflies. How well you execute
Their postures, the wings of the overland dove spread
Like a Japanese fan, the jackdaw frozen
At the moment of his descent into the locust.

It grows easier and easier. Soon the cedar shrike stops
On his own and waits for you, gripped to the fence post.
The grosbeak rests all day on the limb by your page,
And when you picture the rare azure-throated swallow,
He suddenly materializes under the eaves, preparing
His mudball. In the evening before the fire,
As you remember the Réunion solitaire, the giant auk,
They appear in the room, roosting on the ginger jars
Above the mantelpiece. You even wake one morning
To discover that the lark bunting has been nesting

Under your knuckles just as you dreamed he was.
There is a definite stir of preening among your papers.

Tonight, a strange chukal hen has flown to the cornice
Above your window. The invisible grey-green thimble bird
Is slowly coming into sight by your glass, and perched
On the bedpost, an unmarked polar hawk is watching
With his stern golden eye over the entire length of your quilt.

## Suppose Your Father Was a Redbird

Suppose his body was the meticulous layering
Of graduated down which you studied early,
Rows of feathers increasing in size to the hard-splayed
Wine-gloss tips of his outer edges.

Suppose, before you could speak, you watched
The slow spread of his wing over and over,
The appearance of that invisible appendage,
The unfolding transformation of his body to the airborne.
And you followed his departure again and again,
Learning to distinguish the red microbe of his being
Far into the line of the horizon.

Then today you might be the only one able to see
The breast of a single red bloom
Five miles away across an open field.
The modification of your eye might have enabled you
To spot a red moth hanging on an oak branch
In the exact center of the Aurorean Forest.
And you could define for us, "hearing red in the air,"
As you predict the day pollen from the poppy
Will blow in from the valley.

Naturally you would picture your faith arranged
In filamented principles moving from pink
To crimson at the final quill. And the red tremble
Of your dream you might explain as the shimmer
Of his back lost over the sea at dawn.
Your sudden visions you might interpret as the uncreasing
Of heaven, the bones of the sky spread,
The conceptualized wing of the mind untangling.

Imagine the intensity of your revelation
The night the entire body of a star turns red

And you watch it as it rushes in flames
Across the black, down into the hills.

If your father was a redbird,
Then you would be obligated to try to understand
What it is you recognize in the sun
As you study it again this evening
Pulling itself and the sky in dark red
Over the edge of the earth.

# The Rites of Passage

The inner cell of each frog egg laid today
In these still open waters is surrounded
By melanin pigment, by a jelly capsule
Acting as cushion to the falling of the surf,
As buffer to the loud crow-calling
Coming from the cleared forests to the north.

At 77° the single cell cleaves in 90 minutes,
Then cleaves again and in five hours forms the hollow
Ball of the blastula. In the dark, 18 hours later,
Even as a shuffle in the grass moves the shadows
On the shore and the stripes of the moon on the sand
Disappear and the sounds of the heron jerk
Across the lake, the growing blastula turns itself
Inside out unassisted and becomes a gut.

What is the source of the tension instigating next
The rudimentary tail and gills, the cobweb of veins?
What is the impetus slowly directing the hard-core
Current right up the scale to that one definite moment
When a fold of cells quivers suddenly for the first time
And someone says loudly "heart," born, beating steadily,
Bearing now in the white water of the moon
The instantaneous distinction of being liable to death?

Above me, the full moon, round and floating deep
In its capsule of sky, never trembles.
In ten thousand years it will never involute
Its white frozen blastula to form a gut,
Will never by a heart be called born.

Think of that part of me wishing tonight to remember
The split-second edge before the beginning,
To remember by a sudden white involution of sight,

By a vision of tension folding itself
Inside clear open waters, by imitating a manipulation
Of cells in a moment of distinction, wishing to remember
The entire language made during that crossing.

## Without Violence

That cat who comes during sleep, quiet
On his cushioned claws, without violence,
Who enters the house with a low warm rattle
In his throat; that cat who has been said
To crawl into a baby's crib without brushing
The bars, to knit his paws on the pale
Flannel of the infant's nightdress, to settle
In sleep chin to chin with the dear one
And softly steal the child's breath
Without malice, as easily as pulling
A silk scarf completely through a gold ring;

The same cat who has been known to nudge
Through castle doors, to part tent flaps,
To creep to the breasts of brave men,
Ease between their blankets, to stretch
Full length on the satin bodices of lovely
Women, to nuzzle their cheeks with his great
Feline mane; it was that cat who leaped last night
Through the west window of father's bedroom.
Who chose to knead his night's rest on my father's
Shoulder, who slept well, breathing deeply,
Leaving just before dawn to saunter toward
The north, his magnificent tail and rump
Swaying with a listless and gorgeous grace.

# The Question of Affection

We don't know yet what it means to be touched,
To be the recipient of caresses, what the ear
Learns of itself when its lines are followed
By the finger of somebody else.

We know the spine of the infant can expand,
The neck grow sturdy, the shoulder blades facile
By fondling alone. The acuity of the eye is increased,
The lung capacity doubled by random nuzzles
To the ribs.

But we don't understand what the mind perceives
When the thigh's length is fixed by the dawdling
Of the lover's hand, when the girth of the waist
Is defined by the arms of a child.

An affectionate ear on the belly must alter
The conception of the earth pressing itself against the sky.
An elbow bent across the chest must anticipate
Early light angled over the lake. The curl of the pea
Can be understood as one hand caught carefully inside another.

Cores and cylinders, warm boundaries and disappearing curves,
What is it we realize when these interruptions of space
Are identified with love in the touch of somebody else?

I must remember now what it was I recognized
In the sky outside the window last night
As I felt the line of my shoulder drawn
In the trace of your lips.

## Seduced by Ear Alone

Someone should explain how it happens, starting
With the dull stimulation of anvil and stirrups,
The established frequency of shifting air molecules
Initiated by your voice, entering my ear.
The mind, having learned how, can find the single silk
Strand of your breath anywhere, latch on and remember.

But not actually touching the body at all,
How do words alone ease the strictures of the palms,
Alter the tendency of the thighs, cause
The eyes to experience visions? I can see clearly
The stark white sliver of passion running a mile deep
In your whisper.

Maybe the ease of your voice suggests
The bliss of some previous state—sleeping
In a deep crevice at the top of a mountain, the eyes
Sealed tight, or being fed by motion in warm water
At the edge of the sea. By the twist of leaves
In a forest of poplars, I understand how light is fractioned
And born again in the aspects of your words.
I listen like an eddy in deep water turning easily
From one existence to another. I want now
To be covered by you.

And alone on any night, if the wind in the trees
Should sound by accident like the timbre of your voice,
I can be fooled for an instant, feeling suddenly in the dark
Estimable and saved.

*Achieving Perspective*

Straight up away from this road,
Away from the fitted particles of frost
Coating the hull of each chick pea,
And the stiff archer bug making its way
In the morning dark, toe hair by toe hair,
Up the stem of the trillium,
Straight up through the sky above this road right now,
The galaxies of the Cygnus A cluster
Are colliding with each other in a massive swarm
Of interpenetrating and exploding catastrophes.
I try to remember that.

And even in the gold and purple pretense
Of evening, I make myself remember
That it would take 40,000 years full of gathering
Into leaf and dropping, full of pulp splitting
And the hard wrinkling of seed, of the rising up
Of wood fibers and the disintegration of forests,
Of this lake disappearing completely in the bodies
Of toad slush and duckweed rock,
40,000 years and the fastest thing we own,
To reach the one star nearest to us.

And when you speak to me like this,
I try to remember that the wood and cement walls
Of this room are being swept away now,
Molecule by molecule, in a slow and steady wind,
And nothing at all separates our bodies
From the vast emptiness expanding, and I know
We are sitting in our chairs
Discoursing in the middle of the blackness of space.
And when you look at me
I try to recall that at this moment
Somewhere millions of miles beyond the dimness

Of the sun, the comet Biela, speeding
In its rocks and ices, is just beginning to enter
The widest arc of its elliptical turn.

## The Brain Creates Itself

A thread of tissues takes shape
As I first comprehend the red rock crossed twice
By the fringe-toed lizard at dusk.
A unique chain of cells becomes actual
As I identify the man beneath the white beech
And his influence on the nesting kiwi bird.

A new vein of reactions must arise
With my discovery of the dark star
On the rim of Sirius. A split-second network
Must be brought into being as I find the African
Dung beetle's egg buried in the elephant bolus.
And for each unacknowledged aspect of the purple
Spikenard beside the marsh-elder-to-be, for each unrecognized
Function of the ogre-faced stick spider at dawn,
A potential neuron is absent in the frontal lobe.

Imagine the molecular structure I create
As I contemplate the Galapagos dragon
At the bottom of the ocean stopping his heart
At will, dying for three minutes motionless
In the suck and draw of the sea. Imagine,
When I study his rapid zigzag swagger to the surface,
How a permanent line like silver makes its way
From the inner base of my skull to the top of my head.

And as I look at your face, following the contours
From your forehead to your chin, coming back again
To your eyes, I can almost picture the wide cranial
Web developing as my definite affection
For these particulars.

## The Man Hidden Behind the Drapes

When I entered the room and turned on the lights,
There were his feet bare beneath the edge
Of the draperies, his tendons flexed, the bony
Diamonds of his ankles shadowed. If I'd seen
His face I might have laughed.

Remember the naked feet of Christ seen so often,
Washed, kissed, dried in women's hair,
Or crossed and bleeding, pinioned
Like butterfly wings?

When I opened the door,
There were his feet below the drapes, as quiet
As if they lounged beneath a fine robe. Headlights
Moving slowly up the drive at this point
Would have fully exposed his nude body in the window,
His buttocks tensed, his face turned toward the glare
For that moment, then disappearing again into the darkness.

An artist might have pictured snow on the lawn
And a moon and a child looking out from the house
Across the way, watching the figure behind the glass,
The white panes across his back, his hands reaching
For the parting in the curtains.

When I entered the room the light spread first
In a rectangle straight across the floor to his feet,
His toes squeezing under in a crippled kind of gripping.
Someone watching from the end of the hall behind me
Would have seen my body framed in the light of the doorway
And beyond me the wall of the drapes.

Understand the particular axis at which he stood
In the vision of each different beholder, the multiple

Coordinates of hour and position and place coinciding
With the grids of light and sound and preceding
Interpretations. Consider that indeterminable effect
Of his being on the eye of the one unaware of his existence.

There is a house three blocks away that has no man
Behind the drapes. There is a house on a high sea wall
That has two men and no window. There is a house
That does not speak this language and consequently
Tells us nothing.

Almost laughing, my hand still on the door,
I stood watching his feet, and had there been an old woman
Living in the attic, then looking down through a chink in the
        ceiling
She would have seen in two dimensions, the knuckles of his toes,
The top of my head.

## Concepts and Their Bodies
### (The Boy in the Field Alone)

Staring at the mud turtle's eye
Long enough, he sees *concentricity* there
For the first time, as if it possessed
Pupil and iris and oracular lid,
As if it grew, forcing its own gene of circularity.
The concept is definitely
The cellular arrangement of sight.

The five amber grasses maintaining their seedheads
In the breeze against the sky
Have borne *latitude* from the beginning,
Secure *civility* like leaves in their folds.
He discovers *persistence* in the mouth
Of the caterpillar in the same way
As he discovers clear syrup
On the broken end of the dayflower,
Exactly as he comes accidently upon
The mud crown of the crawfish.

The spotted length of the bullfrog leaping
Lakeward just before the footstep
Is not bullfrog, spread and sailing,
But the body of *initiative* with white glossy belly.
*Departure* is the wing let loose
By the dandelion, and it does possess
A sparse down and will not be thought of,
Even years later, even in the station
At midnight among the confusing lights,
As separate from that white twist
Of filament drifting.

Nothing is sharp enough to disengage
The butterfly's path from *erraticism.*

And *freedom* is this September field
Covered this far by tree shadows
Through which this child chooses to run
Until he chooses to stop,
And it will be so hereafter.

## The Determinations of the Scene

Consider one born in the desert,
How he must see his sorrow rise
In the semblance of the yucca spreading
Its thorn-covered leaves in every direction,
Pricking clear to the ends
Of his fingers. He recognizes it
And deals with it thus. He learns to ponder
Like the reptile, in a posed quiet
Of the mind, to move on the barest
Essentials, to solve problems
Like the twisted mesquite sustaining itself.
He puts edges to the nouns of his statements,
Copying the distinct lines of the canyon in shadow
And established cool niches out of the sun
In every part of his dogma. He understands
His ecstasy in terms of fluidity, high spring water
In motion through the arroyo.

That one born in the forest, growing up
With canopies, must seek to secure coverings
For all of his theories. He blesses trees
And boulders, the solid and barely altered.
He is biased in terms of stable growth vertically.
And doesn't he picture his thoughts springing
From moss and decay, from the white sponge
Of fungus and porous toadstools blending?
He is shaped by the fecund and the damp,
His fertile identifications with humus
And the aroma of rain on the deepening
Forest floor. Seeing the sky only in pieces
Of light, his widest definition must be modeled
After the clearing hemmed in by trees.

And consider the child raised near the sea, impinged
Upon constantly by the surf rising in swells,
Breaking itself to permanent particles of mist
Over the cliffs. Did you really think
The constant commotion of all that fury
Would mean nothing in the formation of the vocabulary
Which he chooses to assign to God?
The surge, the explosion must constitute
The underlying dominion unacknowledged
In his approach to the cosmos.

And we mustn't forget to inquire:
Against what kinds of threats must the psyche
Of the Arctic child protect itself in sleep?

## Being of this State

In the entire night sky, in all of the inverted
Slipped-back-upon-itself almost total emptiness
With its occasional faint clusters of pinprick
Fluctuations, there is not one single
Star grateful for its own light.

And on the stalk of blossoming confusion
Outside my door, barrelheads of camelia fistfuls,
There is not one petal that esteems
The ivory ellipse of its own outer edge
Or the molecules of its own scent escaping.

Who can detect a joy of beholding in the golden
Pipe fish filtering among the golden coral
Or in the blue-bred musk ox with its shaggy frost?
Which one among the tattered fungi remembers
The favor of the damp, the gift of decay?

Along the beach the Arctic terns rush forward
Up to their bellies in salt foam and shell-
Shag rolling, but not one is able to bless first
The mole crab it snips up and swallows.

Inside the network of the clearing, among the scritching
And skeetering, the thuz and the tremulous ching,
There is not one insect able to recognize the sound
Of its own beatification. Clinging to the weeds

In the middle of that broad field spread wide
And pressed against the open night, neither those insects,
Nor the hissing grasses, nor the ash-covered moon
Can ever contemplate the importance
Of the invention of praise.

# *Supposition*

Suppose the molecular changes taking place
In the mind during the act of praise
Resulted in an emanation rising into space.
Suppose that emanation went forth
In the configuration of its occasion:
For instance, the design of rain pocks
On the lake's surface or the blue depths
Of the canyon with its horizontal cedars stunted.

Suppose praise had physical properties
And actually endured? What if the pattern
Of its disturbances rose beyond the atmosphere,
Becoming a permanent outline implanted in the cosmos—
The sound of the celebratory banjo or horn
Lodging near the third star of Orion's belt;
Or to the east of the Pleiades, an atomic
Disarrangement of the words,
"How particular, the pod-eyed hermit crab
And his prickly orange legs"?

Suppose benevolent praise,
Coming into being by our will,
Had a separate existence, its purple or azure light
Gathering in the upper reaches, affecting
The aura of morning haze over autumn fields,
Or causing a perturbation in the mode of an asteroid.
What if praise and its emanations
Were necessary catalysts to the harmonious
Expansion of the void? Suppose, for the prosperous
Welfare of the universe, there were an element
Of need involved.

## The Success of the Hunt

There was a white hart that lived in
that forest, and if anyone killed
it, he would be hanged . . .
—Willa Cather, *My Antonia*

He was sighted once in a clearing at dusk, the gold
Grass up to his shoulders and he standing like a pillar
Of salt staring back; seen again from a high ledge,
A motionless dot of white curled like a bloom
In the green below; surprised along a lake shore
At night, taken for an irregular reflection
Of the moon on the surf.

Some looked only for his red eyes, believing
The body could be too easily hidden
By the translucent green of lighted leaves,
That it could sink blue below the water
Or become boundless against the snow, almost invisible,
That it was not white at night.

Some who followed what was presumed to be his trail
Found the purple toadflax said to grow only
From his hoof marks, and some became engulfed
By cecropia moths thought to spring from his urine.
Others testified to the impassable white cliffs
Alleged to be an accumulated battery of his shadows.

Those who lost their way were forced to rediscover
The edible buds of the winter spruce and to use
The fronds of the cycas for warmth, to repeat again
To themselves the directional details of moss,
And part the pampas grasses clear to the earth,
To smell their way east.

But those who followed farthest with the most detail,

Who actually saw the water rising in his hoof prints
And touched the trees still moist where their bark
Had been stripped, those who recognized at the last moment
The prongs of his antlers disappearing over the edge
Of their vision, they were the ones who learned to tell
By the imbalance of their feet on the earth where it was
He slept at night and by their own vertigo how it was he rose
To nip the dogwood twigs above his head. They learned to smell
His odor in their bedclothes and to waken suddenly at night
To the silence of his haunches rubbing on the ash.
Even now they can find the spot where he walked
From the water dripping and trace on their palms
The path of his winter migration. They can isolate
From any direction the eight lighted points
Of his antlers imprinted in the night sky.
And these, who were methodical with the most success,
Always meant to do more than murder.

## The Significance of Location

The cat has the chance to make the sunlight
Beautiful, to stop it and turn it immediately
Into black fur and motion, to take it
As shifting branch and brown feather
Into the back of the brain forever.

The cardinal has flown the sun in red
Through the oak forest to the lawn.
The finch has caught it in yellow
And taken it among the thorns. By the spider
It has been bound tightly and tied
In an eight-stringed knot.

The sun has been intercepted in its one
Basic state and changed to a million varieties
Of green stick and tassel. It has been broken
Into pieces by glass rings, by mist
Over the river. Its heat
Has been given the board fence for body,
The desert rock for fact. On winter hills
It has been laid down in white like a martyr.

This afternoon we could spread gold scarves
Clear across the field and say in truth,
"Sun you are silk."

Imagine the sun totally isolated,
Its brightness shot in continuous streaks straight out
Into the black, never arrested,
Never once being made light.

Someone should take note
Of how the earth has saved the sun from oblivion.

## A Giant Has Swallowed the Earth

What will it do for him, to have internalized
The many slender stems of riverlets and funnels,
The blunt toes of the pine cone fallen, to have ingested
Lakes in gold slabs at dawn and the peaked branches
Of the fir under snow? He has taken into himself
The mist of the hazel nut, the white hairs of the moth,
And the mole's velvet snout. He remembers, by inner
Voice alone, fogs over frozen gray marshes, fine
Salt on the blunt of the cliff.

What will it mean to him to perceive things
First from within—the mushroom's fold, the martin's
Tongue, the spotted orange of the wallaby's ear,
To become the object himself before he comprehends it,
Putting into perfect concept without experience
The din of the green gully in spring mosses?

And when he stretches on his bed and closes his eyes,
What patterns will appear to him naturally—the schematic
Tracings of the Vanessa butterfly in migration, tacks
And red strings marking the path of each mouse
In the field, nucleic chromosomes aligning their cylinders
In purple before their separation? The wind must settle
All that it carries behind his face and rise again
In his vision like morning.

A giant has swallowed the earth,
And when he sleeps now, o when he sleeps,
How his eyelids murmur, how we envy his dream.

## Counting What the Cactus Contains

Elf owl, cactus wren, fruit flies incubating
In the only womb they'll ever recognize.
Shadow for the sand rat, spines
And barbary ribs clenched with green wax.
Seven thousand thorns, each a water slide,
A wooden tongue licking the air dry.

Inside, early morning mist captured intact,
The taste of drizzle sucked
And sunsplit. Whistle
Of the red-tailed hawk at midnight, rush
Of the leaf-nosed bat, the soft slip
Of fog easing through sand held in tandem.

Counting, the vertigo of its attitudes
Across the evening; in the wood of its latticed bones—
The eye sockets of every saint of thirst;
In the gullet of each night-blooming flower—the crucifix
Of the arid.

In its core, a monastery of cells, a brotherhood
Of electrons, a column of expanding darkness
Where matter migrates and sparks whorl,
And travel has no direction, where distance
Bends backward over itself and the ascension
Of Venus, the stability of Polaris, are crucial.

The cactus, containing
Whatever can be said to be there,
Plus the measurable tremble of its association
With all those who have been counting.

## Making a History

The glutinous snail
In silvery motion
Has rubbed his neck
Against his mate's, covered
Her side-slatted orifice
With his own. The newt,
Jumping suddenly forward underwater,
Has twisted and dropped
His pocket of sperm. And in the field
The fritillary, frenzied for orange,
Has skittered straight up and hovered.

The chortle of the Siamese fighting fish
Held upside down by her mate
Has subsided. The dragon fish
Has chewed the tail of his lover,
And the frigate has been swollen
Three times, burgeoning in red.
Bison have risen from their dirt clouds
Blowing. Antlers have entangled, caribou
Collided, cockerels have caught hold,
And the crack of the mountain sheep meeting
Has broken over the arroyo, and the bowerbirds
Have howled and the fruit bats screamed,
And the wild pigs have lain down
In punctuated barking, and the zigzag cocking
Of the stickleback has widened, and alligators
Have spit and strumped, thrashing
In the crumpled reeds. Storks have bent backward
Rooting at heaven with their long beaks banging,
And the alley cat, in guttural moaning,
Has finally been released, bleeding
At the neck, and everyone
Has something to remember.

## On the Existence of the Soul

How confident I am it is there. Don't I bring it,
As if it were enclosed in a fine leather case,
To particular places solely for its own sake?
Haven't I set it down before the variegated canyon
And the undeviating bald salt dome?
Don't I feed it on ivory calcium and ruffled
Shell bellies, shore boulders, on the sight
Of the petrel motionless over the sea, its splayed
Feet hanging? Don't I make sure it apprehends
The invisibly fine spray more than once?

I have seen that it takes in every detail
I can manage concerning the garden wall and its borders.
I have listed for it the comings and goings
Of one hundred species of insects explicitly described.
I have named the chartreuse stripe
And the fimbriated antenna, the bulbed thorax
And the multiple eye. I have sketched
The brilliant wings of the trumpet vine and invented
New vocabularies describing the interchanges between rocks
And their crevices, between the holly lip
And its concept of itself.

And if not for its sake, why would I go
Out into the night alone and stare deliberately
Straight up into 15 billion years ago and more?

I have cherished it. I have named it.
By my own solicitations
I have proof of its presence.

# Synthesizing the Word

The speckled wood butterfly guards his spot of light
On the forest floor. He rests in that circle of sun
Like a powdery flower against the earth, sounding
Its fragrances. He flies in a spiral upward
Against usurpers, settles again on everything good
That he can distinguish. I am trying to find
Your name. I am trying to remember.

In the field after dark, everything has a sound,
The damp gathering under the weeds, the shift
Of the comb-footed spider, the edges of the trees
Against the night. I am aware of what moves across the tops
Of the grasses and keeps on going. I attend to the pauses
Of the grape-skin peepers, the pine crickets. I am trying
To recall your name. I am watching.

The wild wheat, evening-brown and counting, rises
And bends in the ditches by the road. The other side
Of its existence is here in these words. The hair
Of each seed-head, the invisible crack in each sheath,
The wind taking form among the stalks, all have been here
On this page waiting for themselves from the beginning.
I will put together your name. I am adding.

Reminiscence of barn owls and tit-toms, filaments of jackanapes
And iris bands, auras of glassed-in candlelight and unbroken
Spans of snow, the underwater worm slides along the body
Of the Choctaw reed, feeling its presence. I am
Next to where you are. I will use my fingertips. I will use
My belly. I will study long enough to remember your name.

## All the Elements of the Scene

In the upper right-hand corner of this scene is a copse
Of cottonwood (*Populus deltoides*). Each leaf
Like a silver dollar twists on its flattened stalk.
And parallel to the edge of this scene runs
A line of forest, thin dwarf oak, scrub vine,
The smoketree. Leaning to the left of that, a field
Of flat grasses sways, heavy with thorny seeds. Blue
Toadflax and beebalm bend in the wind toward
The bare rim of the pond in the foreground, its lazy
Wash surfaced with the baweedle bug, the raised eyes
Of the leopard frog (*Rana pipiens*). Pickerelweeds
Make hostage of the dragonfly, the nesting mud tortoise.

Here am I in this scene too, my shadow wrinkling
On the water of the pond, my footprints making pools
Along the bank. And all that I say, each word
That I give to this scene is part of the scene. The act
Of each thing identified being linked to its name
Becomes an object itself here. The bumblebee hovers
Near the bitter orange of the mallow weed. That sentence
And this one too are elements of the scene.

This poem, as real as the carp sliding in green
At the bottom of the pond, is the only object
Within the scene capable of discussing both itself
And the scene. The moist, rotting log sinks
Into earth. The pink toothwort sprouts beside it.
The poem of this scene has 34 lines.

And see, reader, you are here also, watching
As the poem speaks to you, as it points out that you
Were present at the very first word. The fact of your
Cognizance here is established as you read this sentence.

Take note of the existence of the words in this scene
As they tell you—the pond is purple; the sun is blocked
In branches below the oak; there are shadows
On this poem; night things are stirring.

## That Song

I will use the cormorant on his rope at night diving
Into the sea, and the fire on the prow, and the fish
Like ribbons sliding toward the green light in the dark.

I will remember the baneberry and the bladderwort
And keep the white crone under the bosackle tree
And the translucent figs and the candelabra burning alone
In the middle of the plains, and the twig girdler,
And the lizard of Christ running over the waves.

I will take the egg bubble on the flute
Of the elm and the ministries of the predacious
Caul beetle, the spit of the iris, the red juice shot
From the eye of the horny toad, and I will use
The irreducible knot wound by the hazel scrub
And the bog myrtle still tangling, and the sea horse
With his delicate horn, the flywheel of his maneuvering.

I will remember exactly each tab folded down
In the sin book of Sister Alleece and each prayer
Hanging in its painted cylinder above the door
And the desert goat at noon facing
The sun to survive.

I will include the brindled bandicoot and the barnacle
Goose and the new birds hatching from mussels
Under the sea and the migrating wildebeests humming
Like organs, moaning like men.

The sand swimmers alive under the Gobi plateau,
The cactus wren in her nest of thorns and the herald
Of the tarantula wasp and each yellow needle
In the spring field rising, everything will be there,
And nothing will be wasted.

## The Fear of Falling

It comes from the tree apes, this instinct
To grasp, to fill the hollow of the hand
And fasten. Emerging from the womb,
How each must have clawed, grabbing before breathing,
Its mother's hairy knee, the slip of her rump.
Imagine the weak, the unimpressed, dropping
Through leaves like stones to the ground below.

The mind has become itself inside the panic
Of bodies falling with fingers spread useless.
How many times in the jerk of sleep
Has the last hand-hold been seen
Disappearing upward like a small bird sucked into space?

Bound to the clenching habit of the fingers, united
With the compulsion of the hands to grasp, the mind
Perceives in terms of possession, recognizing
Its lack from the beginning—the black fur
Of the void, the bowl of the wide belly, the dark
Of that great invented thigh out of reach.

The first need of the brain is to curl
The conceptual knuckles and tighten.
And whether it is on each warm-water crack
At the bottom of the sea or on every maneuver
Of the swamp muskrat or around the grey spiral
Details of forgiveness, the grip of the brain
Is determined not to be negligible.

Here in the wind at the top of these branches
We recognize
The persistent need to take hold of something
Known to be sure-footed.

# Capturing the Scene

With pen and ink, the artist takes care
To be explicit, each board of the covered bridge
Elucidated, each shingle of the roof. The columns
Of the termites and the holes of the borers to be,
He remembers. He is deliberate to denote those specifics
He understands, filling in the blank with the pause
Of the dragonfly, the scratch of the myrtle weed.
He watches to maintain in his lines exactly
That tedious balance between the river in motion
And the river itself. Like wires, he coordinates
The trees and their affinity for disorder.

How skillfully he locates the woodthrush clearing
The last field beyond the hills, and the worn rocks
Along the bank, each with its own specific hump
Against space. He acknowledges the sunken
And the sucked away, the shadows on the far left
Bearing witness to objects still outside the scene.

And notice how he achieves that incandescence of ink
Around the seed pod. He knows that the scream of the jay,
The odor of the sun-dried wood is entirely in his stroke.
Without making a single mark, he executes the heavens.

And hasn't he understood from the beginning where he must
        never
Look directly—into the dark hedgerow on the opposite bank,
Among the crossed sticks of the rushes and the spaces between,
How he must not stare steadily at the long fall
Of the sky below the horizon or probe too deeply that area
Lying between the ink and its line on the paper? He knows
There is that which he must draw blindfolded or not at all.
And before he can give to the scene its final name,

He must first identify every facet of its multiplicity
In detail; he must then turn away his face completely
And remember more.

from

*The Tattooed Lady in the Garden*

## The Pieces of Heaven

No one alone could detail that falling—the immediate
Sharpening and blunting of particle and plane,
The loosening, the congealing of axis
And field, the simultaneous opening and closing
Composing the first hardening of moment when heaven first
    broke
From wholeness into infinity.

No one alone could follow the falling
Of all those pieces gusting in tattered
Layers of mirage like night rain over a rocky hill,
Pieces cartwheeling like the red-banded leg
Of the locust, rolling like elk antlers dropping
After winter, spiraling slowly like a fossil of squid
Twisting to the bottom of the sea, pieces lying toppled
Like bison knees on a prairie, like trees of fern
In a primeval forest.

And no one could remember the rising
Of all those pieces in that moment, pieces shining
Like cottonwood dust floating wing-side up
Across the bottomland, rising like a woman easily
Lifting to meet her love, like the breasting,
The disappearing surge and scattering crest of fire
Or sea blown against rock, bannered like the quills
Of lionfish in their sway, like the whippling stripe
Of the canebrake rattler under leaves.

Who can envision all of heaven trembling
With the everlasting motion of its own shattering
Into the piece called honor and the piece
Called terror and the piece called death and the piece
Tracing the piece called compassion all the way back
To its source in that initial crimp of potential particle

Becoming the inside and outside called matter and space?

And no one alone can describe entirely
This single piece of heaven partially naming its own falling
Or the guesswork forming the piece
That is heaven's original breaking, the imagined
Piece that is its new and eventual union.

## Second Witness

The only function of the red-cupped fruit
Hanging from the red stem of the sassafras
Is to reveal the same shiny blue orb of berry
Existing in me.

The only purpose of the row of hemlocks blowing
On the rocky ridge is to give form to the crossed lines
And clicking twigs, the needle-leaf matrix
Of evergreen motion I have always possessed.

Vega and the ring nebula and the dust
Of the Pleiades have made clear by themselves
The constellations inherent to my eyes.

What is it I don't know of myself
From never having seen a crimson chat at its feeding
Or the dunnart carrying its young? It must be imperative
That I watch the entire hardening of the bud
Of the clove, that I witness the flying fish breaking
Into sky through the sun-smooth surface of the sea.

I ask the winter wren nesting in the clogged roots
Of the fallen oak to remember the multitoned song
Of itself in my ears, and I ask the short-snouted
Silver twig weevil to be particular and the fishhook
Cactus to be tenacious. I thank the distinct edges
Of the six-spined spider crab for their peculiarities
And praise the freshwater eel for its graces. I urge
The final entanglement of blade and light to keep
Its secrecy, and I beg the white-tailed kite this afternoon,
For my sake, to be keen-eyed, to soar well, to be quick
To make me known.

## Her Delight
### After Psalms I:2,3

The tupelo, the blackgum and the poplar,
The overcup oak and the water hickory stand
Along the riverbank being eternal law all day.
They have risen, transforming soil, yielding
To each other, spreading and bending in easy-sun
Contortions, just as their branches decreed they must
During their rising.

Their shadows cast shadow-law this evening
In the long narrow bars of steady black they make
Over the river, being the permanent mathematical
Matrixes they invent relative to the height
Of their ascending trunks.

And the law taking in the soft moisture
Of slow, pervading rivers underground
Is called root. And the root consistently sorting
Ion and mineral by the describable properties
Of its gated skin is called law.

The plum-shaped fruit of the tupelo
Is the rule defining the conformity
To which it shapes itself. The orange berry
Of the possumhaw creates the sugary orange law
Of the sun by which it makes its reality.
Every flattened pit and dark blue drupe and paper-skin
Seed obeys perfectly the commandment it fashions
By becoming itself.

The trees only write the eternal law
Of whatever they have written—the accomplishment
Of the blackgum ordaining autumn red
In the simultaneous commandment of its scarlet leaves;

The accomplishment of the hickory branching
Its leaf in naked, thin-veined everlasting statutes
Of yellow across the sky.

And the woman standing this evening beneath the river trees,
Watching them rise by fissured bark, by husked and hardened
Fruit held high above the water, watching the long bodies
Of their shadows lying unmoved across the current,
She is the easy law that states she must become,
In the hazy, leaf-encroached columns of the evening sun,
Her meditation in this delight.

## Raising the Eyes That High

It always happens, looking up to the tops
Of the sycamores still white and yellow with sunlight
Above the dark river bottom, or bending back to see
The wind, heard first as a caravan of paper horses
In the upper branches of the pines, or following
The flurried lightning bug to where it disappears
Above the parsley haw then catches on again
Even higher, raising the eyes that high,
The body begins to feel again something of significance.

Maybe it's the result of some predisposition
We've inherited from the trees, something in the genes
Promoting a belief in the importance of ascension
Or reaffirming the 70-million-year-old conviction
That stretching one leaf higher might be enough
To finally discover the sky. There's a feeling
In the body of a conviction like that.

Maybe the act of tilting the head backward
To search the sky for Mizar or Draco
Merely flexes the spinal cord at the neck,
Thus doubling the strength of every impulse
Passing there, or maybe sight is actually deepened
When blood flows backward from the eyes,
Or maybe more oxygen, helped by gravity
To the frontal lobe, expands the normal boundaries
Of the perceived heavens.

It might be something as simple as that.
But it's certain, watching the pale-pearl angle
Of the early evening moon, or following the five
Black cowbirds reel across the greying clouds,
Or tracing the easy drift of a cottonwood seed
Slowly rising directly overhead, it's certain,

There's bound to be something new again of power
Astir in the body.

## Love Song

It's all right, together with me tonight,
How your whole body trembles exactly like the locust
Establishing its dry-cymbal quivering
Even in the farthest branch-tip leaves
Of the tree in which it screams.

Lying next to me, it's all right how similar
You become to the red deer in its agitated pacing
On the open plains by the sea, in its sidling
Haunch against haunch, in the final mastery
Of its mounting.

And it's all right, in those moments,
How you possess the same single-minded madness
Of the opened wood poppy circling and circling,
The same wild strength of its golden eye.

It's true. You're no better
Than the determined boar snorgling and rooting,
No better than the ridiculous, ruffled drumming
Of the prairie chicken, no better
Than the explosion of the milkweed pod
Spilling the white furl of the moon deep
In the midnight field. You're completely
Indistinguishable from the enraged sand myrtle
Absurd in its scarlet spread on the rocky bluffs.

But it's all right. Don't you know
This is precisely what I seek, mad myself
To envelope every last drupe and pearl-dropped ovule,
Every nip and cry and needle-fine boring, every drooping,
Spore-rich tassel of oak flower, all the whistling,
Wing-beating, heavy-tipped matings of an entire prairie
Of grasses, every wafted, moaning seed hook

You can possibly manage to bring to me,
That this is exactly what I contrive to take into my arms
With you, again and again.

## The Hummingbird: A Seduction

If I were a female hummingbird perched still
And quiet on an upper myrtle branch
In the spring afternoon and if you were a male
Alone in the whole heavens before me, having parted
Yourself, for me, from cedar top and honeysuckle stem
And earth down, your body hovering in midair
Far away from jewelweed, thistle and bee balm;

And if I watched how you fell, plummeting before me,
And how you rose again and fell, with such mastery
That I believed for a moment *you* were the sky
And the red-marked bird diving inside your circumference
Was just the physical revelation of the light's
Most perfect desire;

And if I saw your sweeping and sucking
Performance of swirling egg and semen in the air,
The weaving, twisting vision of red petal
And nectar and soaring rump, the rush of your wing
In its grand confusion of arcing and splitting
Created completely out of nothing just for me,

Then when you came down to me, I would call you
My own spinning bloom of ruby sage, my funnelling
Storm of sunlit sperm and pollen, my only breathless
Piece of scarlet sky, and I would bless the base
Of each of your feathers and touch the tine
Of string muscles binding your wings and taste
The odor of your glistening oils and hunt
The honey in your crimson flare
And I would take you and take you and take you
Deep into any kind of nest you ever wanted.

## The Power of Toads

The oak toad and the red-spotted toad love their love
In a spring rain, calling and calling, breeding
Through a stormy evening clasped atop their mates.
Who wouldn't sing—anticipating the belly pressed hard
Against a female's spine in the steady rain
Below writhing skies, the safe moist jelly effluence
Of a final exaltation?

There might be some toads who actually believe
That the loin-shaking thunder of the banks, the evening
Filled with damp, the warm softening mud and rising
Riverlets are the facts of their own persistent
Performance. Maybe they think that when they sing
They sing more than songs, creating rain and mist
By their voices, initiating the union of water and dusk,
Females materializing on the banks shaped perfectly
By their calls.

And some toads may be convinced they have forced
The heavens to twist and moan by the continual expansion
Of their lung sacs pushing against the dusk.
And some might believe the splitting light,
The soaring grey they see above them are nothing
But a vision of the longing in their groins,
A fertile spring heaven caught in its entirety
At the pit of the gut.

And they might be right.
Who knows whether these broken heavens
Could exist tonight separate from trills and toad ringings?
Maybe the particles of this rain descending on the pond
Are nothing but the visual manifestation of whistles
And cascading love clicks in the shore grasses.

Raindrops-finding-earth and coitus could very well
Be known here as one.

We could investigate the causal relationship
Between rainstorm and love-by-pondside if we wished.
We could lie down in the grasses by the water's edge
And watch to see exactly how the heavens were moved,
Thinking hard of thunder, imagining all the courses
That slow, clean waters might take across our bodies,
Believing completely in the rolling and pressing power
Of heavens and thighs. And in the end we might be glad,
Even if all we discovered for certain was the slick, sweet
Promise of good love beneath dark skies inside warm rains.

## The Possible Salvation of Continuous Motion

*Adapted from a love letter written by E. Lotter*

*(1872-1930)*

If we could be taken alone together in a driverless
Sleigh pulled by horses with blinders over endless
Uninhabited acres of snow; if the particles
Of our transgression could be left behind us
Scattered across the woodlands and frozen lakes
Like pieces of light scattered over the flashing snow;

If the initiation and accomplishment of our act
In that sleigh could be separated by miles
Of forest—the careful parting begun
Under the ice-covered cedars, the widening and entering
Accomplished in swirls of frost racing along the hills,
The removal and revelation coming beside the seesaw shifting
Of grassheads rustling in the snowy ditches; all the elements
Of our interaction left in a thousand different places—
Thigh against thigh with the drowsy owlets in the trees
Overhead, your face caught for an instant above mine
In one eye of the snow hare;

If the horses could go fast enough across the ice
So that no one would ever be able to say, "Sin
Was committed *here*," our sin being as diffuse
As broken bells sounding in molecules of ringing
Clear across the countryside;

And under the blanket beside you in the sleigh,
If I could watch the night above the flying heads
Of the horses, if I could see our love exploded
Like stars cast in a black sky over the glassy plains
So that nothing, not even the mind of an angel,
Could ever reassemble that deed;

Well, I would go with you right now,
Dearest, immediately, while the horses
Are still biting and strapping in their reins.

## A Daydream of Light

We could sit together in the courtyard
Before the fountain during the next full moon.
We could sit on the stone bench facing west,
Our backs to the moon, and watch our shadows
Lying side by side on the white walk. We could spread
Our legs to the metallic light and see the confusion
In our hands bound up together with darkness and the moon.
We could talk, not of light, but of the facets of light
Manifesting themselves impulsively in the falling water,
The moon broken and re-created instantaneously over and over.

Or we could sit facing the moon to the east,
Taking it between us as something hard and sure
Held in common, discussing the origins of rocks
Shining in the sky, altering everything exposed below.
What should I imagine then, recognizing its light
On your face, tasting its light on your forehead, touching
Its light in your hair?

Or we could sit on the bench to the north,
Buried by the overhanging sycamore,
The moon showing sideways from the left.
We could wonder if light was the first surface
Imprinted with fact or if black was the first
Underlying background necessary for illumination.
We could wonder if the tiny weightless blackbirds
Hovering over our bodies were leaf shadows
Or merely random blankness lying between splashes fallen
From the moon. We could wonder how the dark shadow
From a passing cloud could be the lightest
Indication across our eyes of our recognition of the moon.

Or we could lie down together where there are no shadows at all,
In the open clearing of the courtyard, the moon

At its apex directly overhead, or lie down together
Where there are no shadows at all, in the total blackness
Of the alcove facing north. We could wonder, at the end,
What can happen to light, what can happen to darkness,
When there is no space for either left between us.

We must ask if this daydream is light broken
And re-created instantaneously or simply an impulsive
Shadow passing across the light in our eyes,
Finding no space left for its realization.

# The Definition of Time

In the same moment
That Kioka's great-great-grandfather died,
11,000 particles of frost dissolved into dew
On the blades of the woodrush,
And three water lily leaf beetles paused
Anticipating light making movements
Of their bodies in the weeds.

And in that same moment an earthworm
Swallowed a single red spore down its slimmest
Vein, and the chimney crayfish shoveled a whisker farther
Through slick pond-bottom silt, and one slow
Slice of aster separated its purple segment
From the bud.

Simultaneously the mossy granite along the ridge shifted
Two grains on its five-mile fault, and the hooves
Of ewe and pony, damp in the low-field fog,
Shook with that shift. The early hawk on the post
Blinked a drop of mist from its eye, and the black tern
With a cry flew straight up, remembering the marsh
By scent alone over the sandy hills.

And in that instant the field, carried
Without consent through the dark, held
Its sedges steady for the first turn
Into the full orange sun, and each tense sliver
Of pine on the mountains far to the east
Shone hot already in a white noon,
And in the dark night-sea far behind the field and forest,
The head of a single shark sperm pierced
An ovum and became blood.

The twelfth ring of the tallest redwood

Hardened its circle, and the first lick of the hatching
Goatweed butterfly was made tongue. And Kioka
And his ancestors call the infinite and continuous
Record they make of this moment, "The Book
Of the Beginning and the Chronicle of the End."

## The Possible Suffering of a God During Creation

It might be continuous—the despair he experiences
Over the imperfection of the unfinished, the weaving
Body of the imprisoned moonfish, for instance,
Whose invisible arms in the mid-waters of the deep sea
Are not yet free, or the velvet-blue vervain
Whose grainy tongue will not move to speak, or the ear
Of the spitting spider still oblivious to sound.

It might be pervasive—the anguish he feels
Over the falling away of everything that the duration
Of the creation must, of necessity, demand, maybe feeling
The break of each and every russet-headed grass
Collapsing under winter ice or feeling the split
Of each dried and brittle yellow wing of the sycamore
As it falls from the branch. Maybe he winces
At each particle-by-particle disintegration of the limestone
Ledge into the crevasse and the resulting compulsion
Of the crevasse to rise grain by grain, obliterating itself.

And maybe he suffers from the suffering
Inherent to the transitory, feeling grief himself
For the grief of shattered beaches, disembodied bones
And claws, twisted squid, piles of ripped and tangled,
Uprooted turtles and rock crabs and Jonah crabs,
Sand bugs, seaweed and kelp.

How can he stand to comprehend the hard, pitiful
Unrelenting cycles of coitus, ovipositors, sperm and zygotes,
The repeated unions and dissolutions over and over,
The constant tenacious burying and covering and hiding
And nesting, the furious nurturing of eggs, the bright
Breaking-forth and the inevitable cold blowing-away?

Think of the million million dried stems of decaying

Dragonflies, the thousand thousand leathery cavities
Of old toads, the mounds of cows' teeth, the tufts
Of torn fur, the contorted eyes, the broken feet, the rank
Bloated odors, the fecund brown-haired mildews
That are the residue of his process. How can he tolerate knowing
There is nothing else here on earth as bright and salty
As blood spilled in the open?

Maybe he wakes periodically at night,
Wiping away the tears he doesn't know
He has cried in his sleep, not having had time yet to tell
Himself precisely how it is he must mourn, not having had time
      yet
To elicit from his creation its invention
Of his own solace.

There could be a quirk in the conception of time.
For instance, the brief slide of a single herring
In the sights of an ocean bird might be measured,
At the last moment, in a slow motion of milliseconds,
Each fin spread like a fan of transparent bones
Breaking gradually through the green sea, a long
And complete absorption in that one final movement
Of body and wave together. It could be lengthened
To last a lifetime.

Or maybe there is a strange particulate vision
Only possible in a colony of microscopic copepod
Swaying in and out of the sand eel's range, swallowed
Simultaneously by the thousands. Who knows
What the unseen see? There might be a sense
Of broadcast, a fulfillment of scattering felt
Among the barnacle larva, never achieved
By the predatory shag at the top of the chain.
And the meadow vole crouched immediately below
The barred owl must experience a sudden and unusual
Hard hold on the potential.

Death coming in numbers among the small and uncountable
Might be altered in its aspects. An invaded nest
Of tadpoles might perceive itself as an array of points
Lit briefly in a sparkling pattern of extinction
Along the shore. An endless variety of split-second
Scenes might be caught and held visible in the separate eyes
Of each sea turtle penned on the beach. Death,
Functioning in a thousand specific places at once,
Always completing the magnitude of its obligations,
Has never been properly recognized for its ingenuity.

We must consider the possibility

That from the viewpoint of a cluster of flagellates
We might simply appear to be possessed
By an awkward notion of longevity, a peculiar bias
For dying alone.

# The Verification of Vulnerability: Bog Turtle

Guarded by horned beak and nails, surrounded
By mahogany carapace molded in tiles
Like beveled wood, hidden within the hingeless
Plastron, beneath twelve, yellow-splotched
Black scutes, buried below the inner lungs
And breast, harbored in the far reaches
Of the living heart, there it exists,
As it must, that particle of vulnerability,
As definite in its place as if it were a brief glint
Of steel, buried inside the body of the bog turtle.

And it is carried in that body daily, like a pinpoint
Of diamond in a dark pouch, through marshy fields
And sunlit seepages, and it is borne in that body,
Like a crystal of salt-light locked in a case
Of night, borne through snail-ridden reeds and pungent
Cow pastures in spring. It is cushioned and bound
By folds of velvet, by flesh and the muscle
Of dreams, during sleep on a weedy tussock all afternoon.
It is divided and bequeathed again in June, protected
By thick sap, by yolk meal and forage inside its egg
Encompassed by the walls of shell and nest.

Maybe I can imagine the sole intention present
In the steady movement of turtle breath filled
With the odor of worms this morning, stirring
Clover moisture at the roots. Maybe I can understand
How the body has taken form solely
Around the possibility of its own death,
How the entire body of the bog turtle
Cherishes and maintains and verifies the existence
Of its own crucial point of vulnerability exactly
As if that point were the only distinct,
Dimensionless instant of eternity ever realized.

And maybe I can guess what it is we own,
If, in fact, it is true: the proof of possession
Is the possibility of loss.

I don't know why the horned lizard wants to live.
It's so ugly—short prickly horns and scowling
Eyes, lipless smile forced forever by bone,
Hideous scaly hollow where its nose should be.

I don't know what the horned lizard has to live for,
Skittering over the sun-irritated sand, scraping
The hot dusty brambles. It never sees anything but gravel
And grit, thorns and stickery insects, the towering
Creosote bush, the ocotillo and its whiplike
Branches, the severe edges of the Spanish dagger.
Even shade is either barren rock or barb.

The horned lizard will never know
A lush thing in its life. It will never see the flower
Of the water-filled lobelia bent over a clear
Shallow creek. It will never know moss floating
In waves in the current by the bank or the blue-blown
Fronds of the water clover. It will never have a smooth
Glistening belly of white like the bullfrog or a dew-heavy
Trill like the mating toad. It will never slip easily
Through mud like the skink or squat in the dank humus
At the bottom of a decaying forest in daytime.
It will never be free of dust. The only drink it will ever know
Is in the body of a bug.

And the horned lizard possesses nothing noble—
Embarrassing tail, warty hide covered with sharp dirty
Scales. No touch to its body, even from its own kind,
Could ever be delicate or caressing.

I don't know why the horned lizard wants to live.
Yet threatened, it burrows frantically into the sand
With a surprisingly determined fury of forehead, limbs

And ribs. Pursued, it even fights for itself, almost rising up,
Posturing on its bowed legs, propelling blood out of its eyes
In tight straight streams shot directly at the source
Of its possible extinction. It fights for itself,
Almost rising up, as if the performance of that act,
The posture, the propulsion of the blood itself,
Were justification enough and the only reason needed.

# Eulogy for a Hermit Crab

You were consistently brave
On these surf-drenched rocks, in and out of their salty
Slough holes around which the entire expanse
Of the glinting grey sea and the single spotlight
Of the sun went spinning and spinning and spinning
In a tangle of blinding spume and spray
And pistol-shot collisions your whole life long.
You stayed. Even with the wet icy wind of the moon
Circling your silver case night after night after night
You were here.

And by the gritty orange curve of your claws,
By the soft, wormlike grip
Of your hinter body, by the unrelieved wonder
Of your black-pea eyes, by the mystified swing
And swing and swing of your touching antennae,
You maintained your name meticulously, you kept
Your name intact exactly, day after day after day.
No one could say you were less than perfect
In the hermitage of your crabness.

Now, beside the racing, incomprehensible racket
Of the sea stretching its great girth forever
Back and forth between this direction and another,
Please let the words of this proper praise I speak
Become the identical and proper sound
Of my mourning.

## Trinity

I wish something slow and gentle and good
Would happen to me, a patient and prolonged
Kind of happiness coming in the same way evening
Comes to a wide-branched sycamore standing
In an empty field; each branch, not succumbing,
Not taken, but feeling its entire existence
A willing revolution of cells; even asleep,
Feeling a decision of gold spreading
Over its ragged bark and motionless knots of seed,
Over every naked, vulnerable juncture; each leaf
Becoming a lavender shell, a stem-deep line
Of violet turning slowly and carefully to possess exactly
The pale and patient color of the sky coming.

I wish something that slow and that patient
Would come to me, maybe like the happiness
Growing when the lover's hand, easy on the thigh
Or easy on the breast, moves like late light moves
Over the branches of a sycamore, causing
A slow revolution of decision in the body;
Even asleep, feeling the spread of hazy coral
And ivory-grey rising through the legs and spine
To alter the belief behind the eyes; feeling the slow
Turn of wave after wave of acquiescence moving
From the inner throat to the radiance of a gold belly
To a bone center of purple; an easy, slow-turning
Happiness of possession like that, prolonged.

I wish something that gentle and that careful
And that patient would come to me. Death
Might be that way if one knew how to wait for it,
If death came easily and slowly,
If death were good.

# The Creation of the Inaudible

Maybe no one can distinguish which voice
Is god's voice sounding in a summer dusk
Because he calls with the same rising frequency,
The same rasp and rattling rustle the cicadas use
As they cling to the high leaves in the glowing
Dust of the oaks.

His exclamations might blend so precisely with the final
Crises of the swallows settling before dark
That no one will ever be able to say with certainty,
"That last long cry winging over the rooftop
Came from god."

Breathy and low, the vibrations of his nightly
Incantations could easily be masked by the scarcely
Audible hush of the lakeline dealing with the rocky shore,
And when a thousand dry sheaths of rushes and thistles
Stiffen and shiver in an autumn wind, anyone can imagine
How quickly and irretrievably his whisper might be lost.

Someone faraway must be saying right now:
The only unique sound of his being
Is the spoken postulation of his unheard presence.

For even if he found the perfect chant this morning
And even if he played the perfect strings to accompany it,
Still, no one could be expected to know,
Because the blind click beetle flipping in midair,
And the slider turtle easing through the black iris bog,
And two savannah pines shedding dawn in staccato pieces
Of falling sun are already engaged in performing
The very same arrangement themselves.

## Transformation

When the honeysuckle vine blooming beside the barn
First became the white and yellow tangle of her eye,
And the mouse snake passing beneath the dry grasses
Became the long steady hush of her ear, and the spring hill
Was transformed into the rise of her bare feet climbing in April.

When the afternoon between the canyon walls
Became the echoing shout of her voice, and the line
Of orange-stone sun, appearing through a crevice
Of granite, shone as the exact hour of her solstice;
When the cold January wind turned to the flesh
Of her stinging fingertips, and the birds flying
Over the rice beds became the seven crows of her count;

When the dawning sun was the beginning rim
Of light showing over the eastern edge of her sight,
And the earth became, for the only time in its history,
The place of her shadow, and the possibilities
Lying faraway between the stars were suddenly
The unwitnessed boundaries of her heart . . .

Felicia was born.

# Intermediary

For John A. and Arthur

This is what I ask: that if they must be taken
They be taken like the threads of the cotton grass
Are taken by the summer wind, excited and dizzy
And safe, flying inside their own seeds;
And if they must be lost that they be lost
Like leaves of the water starwort
Are lost, submerged and rising over and over
In the slow-rooted current by the bank.

I ask that they always be found
With the same sure and easy touch
The early morning stillness uses to find itself
In needles of dew on each hyssop in the ditch.

And may they see everything the boatman bug,
Shining inside its bubble of air, sees
Through silver skin in the pond-bottom mud,
And may they be obliged in the same way the orb snail,
Sucking on sedges in shallow water, is obliged.
And may they be promised everything a single blade
Of sweet flag, kept by the grip of the elmid
On its stem, kept by the surrounding call
Of the cinnamon teal, kept by its line
In the marsh-filled sky, is promised.

Out loud, in public and in writing, I ask again
That solace come to them like sun comes
To the egg of the longspur, penetrating the shell,
Settling warmth inside the potential heart
And beginnings of bone. And I ask that they remember
Their grace in the same way the fetal bird remembers light
Inside the blackness of its gathering skull inside
The cave of its egg.

And with the same attention a streamer of ice
Moving with the moon commands, with the same decision
The grassland plovers declare as they rise
From the hayfields into the evening sky,
I ask that these pleas of mine arrest the notice
Of all those angels already possessing a lasting love
For fine and dauntless boys like mine.

Albert, standing at the window, began by saying,
"False china eggs in a chicken's nest stimulate
The hen to lay eggs that are real,
And they also occasionally fool weasels."

"Telling the truth to a chicken then"
Replied Sonia, "must be considered a grievous sin,
And deception, in this case, an extraordinary virtue."

"Chickens, brooding on china eggs as well as real ones,"
Said Cecil, rubbing his chin, "might regard glass eggs
As admirably false, but a weasel nosing the nest
Would consider glass eggs a malevolent tomfoolery
And the devil's own droppings."

"A weasel, testing the reality of eggs,
Must find glass and albumen
Equally easy to identify," continued Albert.

"China eggs, whether warm or not," said Felicia,
Mocking herself in the mirror, "at least consistently maintain
Their existence as false eggs."

"Perhaps the true egg, unable to maintain its reality
For long, is actually a weak imitation
Of the eternal nature of the glass egg," said Albert,
Drawing his initials on the frost windowpane.

"Someone must investigate how the real image
Of a false egg in the chicken's true eye causes the cells
Of a potential egg to become an actuality," said Gordon,
Laying his book on the table.

"Can we agree then that the false china egg,

A deceptive but actual instigator,
Is the first true beginning of the chicken yard?"
Asked Sonia, filling in the last line of the game sheet.

Albert, rushing outdoors to discover
What the dogs had cornered in the brush beside the barn,
Found a weasel in the snow
With bloody yolk on its whiskers and a broken tooth.

# Finding the Tattooed Lady in the Garden

Circus runaway, tattooed from head to toe in yellow
Petals and grape buds, rigid bark and dust-streaked
Patterns of summer, she lives naked among the hedges
And bordered paths of the garden. She hardly
Has boundaries there, so definite is her place.

Sometimes the golden flesh of the butterfly,
Quiet and needled in the spot of sun on her shoulder,
Can be seen and sometimes the wide blue wing
Of her raised hand before the maple and sometimes
The crisscrossed thicket, honeysuckle and fireweed,
Of her face. As she poses perfectly, her legs apart,
Some people can find the gentian-smooth meadow-skin showing
Through the distant hickory groves painted up her thighs
And the warm white windows of open sky appearing
Among the rose blossoms and vines of her breasts.

Shadow upon tattooed shadow upon real shadow,
She is there in the petaled skin of the iris
And the actual violet scents overlapping
At the bend of her arm, beneath and beyond
The initial act announcing the stems
Of the afternoon leafed and spread
In spires of green along her ribs, the bronze
Lizard basking at her navel.

Some call her searched-for presence the being
Of being, the essential garden of the garden.
And some call the continuing postulation
Of her location the only underlying structure,
The single form of flux, the final proof
And presence of crafted synonymy.
And whether the shadows of the sweetgum branches
Above her shift in the breeze across her breasts

Or whether she herself sways slightly
Beneath the still star-shaped leaves of the quiet
Forest overhead or whether the sweetgum shadows
Tattooed on her torso swell and linger
As the branches above are stirred by her breath,
The images possessed by the seekers are one
And the same when they know them as such.

And in the dark of late evening,
Isn't it beautiful the way they watch for her
To turn slowly, displaying the constellations
Penned in light among the black leaves
And blossoms of her back, the North Star
In its only coordinates shining at the base
Of her neck, the way they study the first glowing
Rim of the moon rising by its own shape
From the silvered curve of her brilliant hip?

# Reaching the Audience

*from the introduction*

*to the First Book of Iridaceae.*

We will start with a single blue dwarf iris
Appearing as a purple dot on a hairstreak
Butterfly seen in a distant pine barrens and proceed
Until we end with a single point of purple spiraling
Like an invisible wing in the center of the flower
Making fact.

We will investigate a stand of blue flags crimsoned
By the last sun still showing over the smoky edges
Of the ravine and illustrate in sequence the glazing
Of those iris by the wet gold of an early dawn.

We will survey a five-mile field of purple iris
Holding bristle-legged insects under the tips
Of their stamens and measure the violet essence
Gathered at the bases of their wings and devote
One section to a molecule of iris fragrance
Preserved and corked in a slender glass.

There will be a composition replicating the motion
Of the iris rolling sun continually over its rills
And another for the stillness of the iris sucking ivory
Moonlight through its hollows making ivory roots.

There will be photographs in series of the eyes
Of a woman studying the sepals of an iris
In a lavender vase and a seven-page account of the crested
Iris burning at midnight in the shape of its flame
And six oriental paintings of purple petals torn apart
And scattered over snow beneath birches and a poem
Tracing a bouquet of blue iris tied together like balloons
Floating across the highest arc of a spring heaven.

There will be an analysis of the word of the iris
In the breath of the dumb and an investigation
Of the touch of the iris in the fingertips of the blind
And a description of the iris-shaped spaces existing
In the forest before the forest became itself
And a delineation of those same blade-thin spaces
Still existing after the forest has been lost again.

It is the sole purpose of these volumes-in-progress
To ensure that anyone stopped anywhere in any perspective
Or anyone caught forever in any crease of time or anyone
Left inside the locked and folded bud of any dream
Will be able to recognize something on these pages
And remember.

# Discovering Your Subject

Painting a picture of the same shrimp boat
Every day of your life might not be so boring.
For a while you could paint only in the mornings,
Each one different, the boat gold in the new sun
On your left, or the boat in predawn fog condensing
Mist. You might have to wait years, rising early
Over and over, to catch that one winter morning when frost
Becomes a boat. You could attempt to capture
The fragile potential inherent in that event.

You might want to depict the easy half-circle
Movements of the boat's shadows crossing over themselves
Through the day. You could examine every line
At every moment—the tangle of nets caught
In the orange turning of evening, the drape of the ropes
Over the rising moon.

You could spend considerable time just concentrating
On boat and birds—Boat with Birds Perched on Bow,
Boat with Birds Overhead, Shadows of Birds Covering
Hull and Deck, or Boat the Size of a Bird,
Bird in the Heart of the Boat, Boat with Wings,
Boat in Flight. Any endeavor pursued long enough
Assumes a momentum and direction all its own.

Or you might decide to lie down one day behind a clump
Of marsh rosemary on the beach, to see the boat embedded
In the blades of the saltwort or show how strangely
The stalk of the clotbur can rise higher than the mast.
Boat Caught like a Flower in the Crotch of the Sand Verbena.

After picturing the boat among stars, after discovering
The boat as revealed by rain, you might try painting
The boat in the eye of the gull or the boat in the eye

Of the sun or the boat in the eye of a storm
Or the eye trapped in the window of the boat.
You could begin a series of self-portraits—The Boat
In the Eye of the Remorseful Painter, The Boat in the Eye
Of the Blissful Painter, The Boat in the Eye of the Blind Painter,
The Boat in the Lazy Painter Forgetting His Eye.

Finally one day when the boat's lines are drawn in completely,
It will begin to move away, gradually changing its size,
Enlarging the ocean, requiring less sky, and suddenly it might
        seem
That you are the one moving. You are the one altering space,
Gliding easily over rough surfaces toward the mark
Between the ocean and the sky. You might see clearly,
For the first time, the boat inside the painter inside the boat
Inside the eye watching the painter moving beyond himself.
You must remember for us the exact color and design of that.

## Being Accomplished

Balancing on her haunches, the mouse can accomplish
Certain things with her hands. She can pull the hull
From a barley seed in paperlike pieces the size of threads.
She can turn and turn a crumb to create smaller motes
The size of her mouth. She can burrow in sand and grasp
One single crystal grain in both of her hands.
A quarter of a dried pea can fill her palm.

She can hold the earless, eyeless head
Of her furless baby and push it to her teat.
The hollow of its mouth must feel like the invisible
Confluence sucking continually deep inside a pink flower.

And the mouse is almost compelled
To see everything. Her hand, held up against the night sky,
Can scarcely hide Venus or Polaris
Or even a corner of the crescent moon.
It can cover only a fraction of the blue moth's wing.
Its shadow could never mar or blot enough of the evening
To matter.

Imagine the mouse with her spider-sized hands
Holding to a branch of dead hawthorn in the middle
Of the winter field tonight. Picture the night pressing in
Around those hands, forced, simply by their presence,
To fit its great black bulk exactly around every hair
And every pinlike nail, forced to outline perfectly
Every needle-thin bone without crushing one, to carry
Its immensity right up to the precise boundary of flesh
But no farther. Think how the heavy weight of infinity,
Expanding outward in all directions forever, is forced,
Nevertheless, to mold itself right here and now
To every peculiarity of those appendages.

And even the mind, capable of engulfing
The night sky, capable of enclosing infinity,
Capable of surrounding itself inside any contemplation,
Has been obliged, for this moment, to accommodate the least
Grasp of that mouse, the dot of her knuckle, the accomplishment
Of her slightest intent.

## Inside God's Eye

As if his eye had no boundaries, at night
All the heavens are visible there. The stars drift
And hesitate inside that sphere like white seeds
Sinking in a still, dark lake. Spirals of brilliance,
They float silently and slowly deeper and deeper
Into the possible expansion of his acuity.
And within that watching, illumination like the moon
Is uncovered petal by petal as a passing cloud clears
The open white flowers of the shining summer plum.

Inside god's eye, light spreads as afternoon spreads,
Accepting the complications of water burr and chestnut,
The efforts of digger bee and cuckoo bee. Even the barest
Light gathers and concentrates there like a ray
Of morning reaching the thinnest nerve of a fairy shrimp
At the center of a pond. And like evening, light
Bends inside the walls of god's eye to make
Skywide globes of fuchsia and orange, violet-tipped
Branches and violet-tinged wings set against a red dusk.

Lines from the tangle of dodder, bindweed
And honeysuckle, from the interweaving knot
Of seaweed and cones, patterns from the network
Of blowing shadow and flashing poplar, fill
And define the inner surface moment of his retina.

And we, we are the only point of reversal
Inside his eye, the only point of light
That turns back on itself and by that turning
Saves time from infinity and saves motion
From obscurity. We are the vessel and the blood
And the pulse he sees as he sees the eye watching
The vision inside his eye in the perfect mirror
Held constantly before his face.

from

*Legendary Performance*

## Naked Boys on Naked Ponies

They ride through invisible hollows
And along the indefinite edges of marshy streams,
Fog swirling up to their ears
Over beds of sida and flowering spurge.
The ponies' withers become ivory with pollen
From the blossoming quince, and the bare
Legs of the boys are marked by flickertail
Barley and wild mint. Moisture
On the corn cockle along the ridges
Makes constant suns in their eyes.

Galloping through forests and across fields
Of drying grasses, this is what they create
By themselves—spilled ginseng and screeching
Pipits, dusts rising from the witherod
And the wild raisin, an effusion of broken
Beargrass somersaulting skyward
And mouse-ear chickweed kicked high.

And beside the river they see themselves
On the opposite bank following themselves
Through water chestnuts and willow oak, and they see
Themselves threading among the stand of hornbeam
In the forest ahead. Watching from the precipice
Above the canyon at evening, they know the bronze
Ponies and their riders curving in a line
Along the ledges below.

And at night they see themselves riding upside down
Across the sky, hair and tails and manes
Dragging in the grasses among the long horn beetles
And burrowing owls. And they see themselves galloping
Across the prairie turned upside down, hair
And tails and manes dragging in the dusty glow

Of the starry nebulae. They know they are the definite
Wish of all unexplored spaces to be ponies and boys.

I tell you the speed of the ponies depends absolutely
On the soaring of the rider squeezing tightly
Inside each of their skulls. And the wings of the boys
Depend absolutely on the flight of the ponies
Galloping across the prairies contained in their bones.
And the soaring of the prairies depends absolutely
On the wings of the ponies squeezing tightly
Inside every grass and bone found in the flight of the boys.

And who cares where they are going,
And who cares if they are real or not,
When their ride by itself is that glorious?

# A Seasonal Tradition

Felicia's music teacher gives a concert for Sonia,
Cecil, Albert, Gordon and Felicia and her insane uncle
In the front parlor every holiday season.
After her traditional repertoire she always plays
One piece on her violin in a register so high
The music can't be heard.

The silence of the parlor during that piece
Is almost complete, broken only by the sputter
Of a candle, a creaking yawn from one of the dogs.

Albert admires the entranced look
On the music teacher's face and the curious trembling
Form of her fingers as she plays. He thinks
He can hear the unheard music in the same way he can hear
Wind among the black strings of the icy willows blowing
In the tundra night. He thinks the silence he hears
Is the same silence found in the eyes of the frogs living
Below the mud at the bottom of the frozen bays.

With tears in her eyes, Felicia says the unheard song
Reminds her of the cries of unborn rice rats
And bog lemmings buried in the winter marsh
And the humming of the white hobblebush blossom still
In its seed and the trill of the unreal bird discovered
In the river trees by the river sun.

Watching the violinist swaying in her velvet gown,
Closing her eyes, pursing her lips, Cecil knows
Sonia is the only possible theme of this composition.

Hoping for a cure for Felicia's uncle, Sonia thinks
The inaudible music might be the unspoken speech
In which he is thought to have lost himself years ago.

At the conclusion of the piece (signaled
By the lowering of the violin) there is always spontaneous
Applause and much barking and leaping by the dogs.

The unheard composition is the one song
Most discussed later over tea and pastries,
And, although it was the subject of the quarrel
During which Cecil knocked Albert's doughnut
From his hand last year, it is still generally considered
The evening's greatest success.

# The Mirror of Pierrot

*For Felicia and the unrealized soul*
*of her favorite lost doll.*

He should never have been set down all alone
In the field like that, a real clown in his floppy
Satin pajamas, dizzy among the trembling pipewort,
Quavering like the brainless wool grass.
Bone-bald in his black skull cap, perpetual
Astonishment on his white painted face, he sits
And stares, his dark lashes as large as teardrops
Circling each wide eye.

How can he ignore the big clicking buttons
Swinging on his baggy blouse as he bends to pick
A prickly daisy for his lapel, or his long cuffs
Falling into the creek as he studies the bravado
Of a crawdad backing under a leaf? Tripped
On the hill by his own pantaloons, he's already lost
One of his tassel-topped silk slippers in a hedgehog hole.

And the starched ruffle around his neck scratches
His ear as he turns to count the jays screaming
Their nonsense among the awkward oaks. He's been teased
For half an hour by a light-headed butterfly flitting
Just out of reach above the raspberry blooms.

Recognizing himself, doesn't he see the wild pantaloons
On the catapulting locust, the bone-tight caps
Of the blackbirds, the white painted faces of the trillium?
He knows the figure he makes sprawled
Among the addle-headed grasses, beside the dumb-struck
Rocks, bewildered under the blank and foolish sky.
He's certain the field is a clumsy buffoon.

Oh, if he could only remember or if he could only

Forget or if he could only imagine someone
Out of sight beyond the hill,
Someone who thinks about him always,
Without laughing.

## The Study of the Splinter Expert

An expert on splinters was the guest lecturer
Featured at the academy last week. His career began
As a youthful hobby—a curiosity concerning
The minute lines in slivers of oak and ash, an expanding
Collection of glass splinters, purple, scarlet;
Metal shavings.

Spending two years as a student sorting
Through the refuse left from the explosion
Of a single pine, deciphering patterns in that tangled
Fall of feathered wood, he discovered and classified
Fifty varieties of splinters broken from splinters.

His meticulous investigation of the calls
Of the meadowlark splintering the spring afternoon
Led to his first book, *The Splinters of Time.*
Since then he has completed research on the splinters
Of moonlight made by the needles of icy firs, wind
Splintering the silver surface of the lake, the splintering
Of the wind by the blades of the bur reed.

In any entity he can only see the underlying
Truth of its splintered reality—the red
And yellow splinters composing rattle box
And hibiscus blooms, splinters forming
In the fertile egg of the swamp snake, the potential
Splinters of chill in future snow. He predicts
The eventual development of an instrument able to locate
And describe each splinter of space.

Concerned with the splintering action of analysis itself,
He has carefully studied photographs of himself
Taken as he scrutinized shavings from the femurs
Of unborn calves, shatters of hickory found

Before the rising of the sap. He has attempted
To locate in his own eye that splinter of light
Creating the original concept of "splinter."

Thursday evening he lectured on his recent
Proposal that the sharpest, most painful
Splinter experienced is not of micromagnesium
Or glass silk but the splinter of pure hypothesis.

A well-known seer has predicted that the death
Of this expert will come by steel splinter piercing
His eye and brain, whereby he will enter that coveted state—
The perfect union of object and idea.

Felicia, infatuated with the erudite demeanor
Of the splinter expert, hasn't left her bed during the five days
Since his departure. She is using a calculator to count
The splinters of loss filling the distance multiplying
Between them, and she's afraid that, should she rise,
The splinters of her despair, blending like moonlight
On the floor, would scatter like dust and be lost forever.

Within the crystal bird that Felicia is admiring
In the window of the curio shop this morning
Is a perfect skeleton of glass bones. The moment
Of the bird's intention to fly appears as a bend
Of purple light curved deep within its wing.
And beneath its glass clavicle is a dram
Of salt water wavering and shimmering like a heart.

As Felicia looks closer she can see, inside the bubble
Of the bird's body, a transparent egg holding a perfect curl
Of unborn bird, its bones folded as glistening wing
And femur of glass threads. Beneath the vestige of clavicle
There is a sure but wavering salt-point of light.

Looking further she can see, within the loins
Of that unborn bird, a semblance of egg containing
A skeleton of spider-bird bones, a shimmer
Of purple veins connected like night and a hair-bone
Of light forming as heaven's intention to rise like a wing.

And inside the glistening drop of potential egg floating
Inside that embryo-to-be nestled inside the unborn
Bird folded inside the glass bird inside the shop window,
Felicia can sense a definite breath of bones, a waver
Of night wing and a microscopic explosion of light rising
In her eye as proof of the intention
Of a non-existent heart to see.

Felicia is counting backwards now to discover
How many deaths and how many births will be needed
To fully release that flight.

No one knows where the shop owner finds
Such curios to display behind his window

Or how he locates the glassblower
Who executes them.

## Gentlemen of Leisure

Yesterday Felicia put an invitation
In the evening newspaper addressed
To all true Gentlemen of Leisure:

> Please come tomorrow for an afternoon
> Of sedate conversation, coffee,
> Mints and finger croissants.

As the gentlemen arrive, ringing
Once at mid-afternoon, all is prepared.
They place their kid gloves, their chapeaux
And their canes, without clatter, on the marble stand
And proceed to the parlor to seat themselves
On the couch of bruised-rose brocade, the white-lacquered
Chairs and the maroon-cushioned settee.

Felicia thinks the Gentlemen of Leisure
Are magnificently regal in their lavender
Lamb's wool suits and pearl buttons. She adores
Their subtle aromas of unsmoked tobacco, crushed marjoram
And black cinnamon stem.

There are prolonged silences in the parlor
As the gentlemen nod to one another and muse
And abstractly balance their demitasse. They touch
Their temples occasionally with the lace
Of their wine-colored cravats.

They discuss for a moment the brief verse
They discussed during their visit last year.
And they note the shadow of the fern
In its bamboo stand on the dark polished floor.
They recall the rare virgin canary
Which eats small white seeds in the forest
And sips single drops of silver water

In the afternoon and again at dawn.

All true Gentlemen of Leisure are genuinely
And exquisitely calm inside the outer trappings
Of their serenity. Unlike Eduard, who hypocritically
Preaches the code common to all Gentlemen of Leisure,
They know nothing personally of biological
Petulance or preordained harangue.

Cecil wants to paint a portrait
Of the gentlemen sitting and gazing together
In the parlor, but he cannot find the proper shade
Of mauve. And he feels, besides, that the vulgar
Movements of his brush might irreparably violate
The sensitivities of his subjects.

This afternoon, Kioka has insisted
On erecting his sweat-bath tipi on the lawn
Beside the parlor windows. Even though Felicia closes
The drapes, Kioka can still be heard chanting
In the sizzling and sputtering steam that rises
From the glowing rocks. What a triumph
That only one teaspoon rattles against its saucer
As Kioka rushes suddenly from his bath
Screaming his surrender and runs toward the lake!

Doesn't each Gentleman of Leisure sleep well at night,
Cool and scented with rosebay on the smoothest white
Linen, under a coverlet of combed angora, a low light
Burning by his bed in a cut-crystal bowl all night?

Sonia must pray for all true Gentlemen of Leisure
Who lend such glorious affirmation
To passivity.

When they rise to leave, precisely

At the perfect moment of dusk, they hold
Their carved canes lightly and stroll
On the white-pebbled path, slowly through the fog
Just gathering among the budding laurel and the full-flowered
Plum, glancing once this way and once that,
And Felicia holds her breath for the beauty.

## The Pursuit as Solution

Whenever Albert is bored, he says he wants to know
What's on the other side of the mind. He says
He sometimes has a vision of himself entering
A bird's throat without injuring it, descending
Deeper and deeper headfirst into that warm black center
Until the pressure building at his feet begins to pull
The whole meadow in behind him, every hop clover
And feather foil and smartweed and swamp candle.
And then the hills follow with their grey-green rocks,
Their shagbarks, bitternuts, sourwoods and birches.
And the iron fence around the lawn and the latticed
Arbor house are sucked in too and the warm perfume
Of guests for dinner, crystal salt shakers,
Embroidered napkins. The whole evening sky
Is taken as if it were a net filled with lapping honey bees,
Bot flies, horntails, shrikes and scaups. And even his dreams
Of flying wingless into space and the invisible and the unlikely
And finally light itself are funnelled in. Then the bird,
In that vacuum remaining, begins to enter its own throat,
Followed by Albert himself diving in behind himself
And Albert's mind turned inside out.

Sonia thinks Albert should pick
One small thing such as a ceramic thimble
Or a brass button from his great-great-granduncle's
Naval uniform or a six-spotted fishing spider
And try to find the other side of that first,
For practice.

Albert is happy with this suggestion, and now,
On this Tuesday afternoon, he isn't bored any longer
But is out searching along the seashore for a perfect
Short-spined sea urchin or a spiral-tufted
Bryozoan or a trumpet worm or a sea mouse

With which to begin.

Gordon says this whole idea is ridiculous.
Once Albert *knows* what's on the other side of his mind,
It won't be on the other side any longer.

## The Love of Enchantment: Felicia Was Kissed in the Garden Last Night

Someone unseen behind her in the sage
And iris odors of the gravel pathway
Definitely took her by the shoulders,
Pushed her hair aside carefully and kissed her
With decision and concern just once,
There at the darkness below her ear.

And there was breath in that kiss
As if the hesitation and impetuosity
Of spring together had finally found
One motion. And there was love
In that motion as when the parting
And reconciliation inside a hawthorn seed
Finally divine together a branch
Full of blossoms.

And now, by her belief in the imagined spell
Created by that kiss, Felicia clearly perceives
The means by which the earth can be taut
With Indian pipe, heavy with matted roots
Of salt marshes, dark with redwood shadows,
While at the same moment it can soar, clean
And shining, a white grain sailing
In the black heavens around the sun.

A new resiliency has risen in Felicia's bones
Since her encounter in the garden, a warm
And dominant, marrow-related alloy sustained
By her spine remembering those fingertips brushing
Her shoulders with praise. Everyone recognizes
The new buoyancy of esteem in the charmed energy
And sureness of her body swimming across
The lily-bordered lake this evening.

Now even Gordon wants to see and touch
That small exalted, transfigured,
Lip-defined, miraculous moment of her neck.

And no one is sorry that, even if just once,
Felicia was kissed and cherished that way
In an ordinary garden rightly declared, rightly
Proclaimed, justifiably announced by Felicia, running
To clasp both of Albert's hands in her own,
As grandly enchanted last night.

## How the Whale Forgets the Love of Felicia

If he breaches at all, he only rises
To a moderate height, rolls little
And falls without luster or surf, silently
In an unremarkable mid-autumn fog.

He rejects the underlying form
Of the fairy shrimp, will not ingest
Fleeing krill if their silver bodies sparkle,
Ignores the possibilities in the strong,
White wings of the manta ray.

In order to avoid the awareness
Of her absence, he must not close his eyes.
In order to avoid the sound of her name,
He must not remind himself to forget.

He deliberately pulls away and bypasses
Brilliant bars of green sun shimmering
Through the dark sea, and he pulls away and sinks
Deliberately from the light salt-vacancies
Of stars ascending like tiny jewels of air
Through the ocean night.

And he never pictures the beauty of barefoot
Riders on horseback when white gulls perch
And flutter on his crusty hump.
And he never remembers tireless dancers
In transparent silks when white waves leap,
Reaching and bowing before a violet sky.

As he moves forward, he doesn't heed or acknowledge
The only direction manifested naturally and forever
Inside the tough hide of his heart, and he doesn't name
The honor of his own broad brow or the honor

Of the comb jellies he passes or the bravery of the bream
And the halfbeaks or the cruelty of the moon's soft skin
Sliding along his own in the night.

How careful he must be never to profess with fervor
The devotion of denial, the clear affirmation
Of suffering.

Indifferent to his own methods, he merely dives
Repeatedly to a depth of dull twilight
Where he meditates without passion on the great
Indeterminable presence of the steady sea, the rock
And return, the capture and simultaneous release
Of its thousand, thousand meaningless caresses.

## *The Myth:* Raison d'Être

Some say there are wild white ponies
Being washed clean in a clear pool
Beneath a narrow falls in the middle
Of the deciduous forest existing
At the center of the sun.

Some say the thrashing of those ponies
Straining against their bridles, the water flying
From their stamping hooves in fiery pieces
And streaks rising higher than the sandbar willows
Along the bank, drops whirling like sparks
From the manes of their shaking heads,
And the shouting and splashing of the boys
Yanked off their feet by the ponies
As they attempt to wash the great shoulders
And rumps of those rearing beasts, as they lather
Their necks and breasts, stroking them,
Soothing them—all this is the source
Of the fierce binding and releasing energy
Existing at the core of the sun.

The purple jays, mad with the chaos,
Shrieking in the tops of the planetrees,
The rough-winged swallows swerving back
And forth in distress, the struggle of the boys
To soap the inner haunch, to reach
Beneath the belly, to dodge the sharp
Pawing hooves, the wide-eyed screaming
Of the slipping ponies being maneuvered
For the final rinse under the splattering falls—
All the fury of this frightening drama,
Some believe, is contained and borne steadily
Across the blue sky strictly by the startling
Light and combustion of its own commotion.

But when those ponies stand, finally quiet,
Their pure white manes and tails braided
With lilac and rock rose, the boys asleep
On their backs, when they stand,
Fragrant and shimmering, their forelocks
Damp with sweet oil, serene and silent
In the motionless dark of the deep
Riverside forest, then everyone can
Easily see and understand the magnificent
Silhouette, the restrained power, the adorned,
Unblemished and abiding beauty
That is the night.

## The Creation of Sin

Gordon wants to commit a sin
Never committed before. He says he is bored
By the lascivious; he has slept through
A thousand adulteries. He calls theft
And murder and greed embarrassingly unimaginative.

He spends an hour each clear afternoon
On the lawn beneath the alders, grooming the dogs,
Trying to imagine a sin so novel
It has not yet been forbidden.

Sometimes, in the moment just before he discerns
The fish treading in light at the bottom
Of the spring or when he studies the eye
Of the short-eared owl in the instant before it sees
The shrew, he is certain he has already committed
That peculiar sin without knowing it. In the early morning,
As he watches himself from the icy black cedars
By the window, dreaming in his sleep, he can almost
Define it.

As the sole author of a sin,
Gordon knows he would be obligated to create
Its expiation by himself. Grace by seaside scrutiny
He might claim, forgiveness by clam classification,
Confession by continual shell collection.
He could invent sacred vows—sworn custodian
Of conifers, promised caretaker of ambush bugs
And toad bugs. He could preach atonement by paper
And mathematics, redemption by ritual
Guessing at the matter of stars.

Today he has recorded a unique grassland prayer
On a tape with the whooping cranes. He has gathered

Sacraments of metamorphic meal moths and hardening
Sassafras fruit. And he knows if he could just commit
A truly original sin, it would mean the beginning
Of his only real salvation.

# One in Three

Although Sonia believes her friend, Lettina,
Is a girl visiting from a coastal city, Kioka
Knows a tree that was once a figurehead
Named Lettina. It stands now in the forest on a rising
Hillside like a wooden girl standing upright on the bow
Of a ship, her skirts blowing around her legs
In soft-leafed branches like the pale green
Billowing remembered by a tree sailing
Like a girl through a forest spring.

Consequently, Kioka believes he is the only one
Who knows how to see the depth of the ocean
In the dark seed-point of Lettina's eyes. And he can hear
The salt swelling in the full leaf forming the circumference
Of her heart. He can find the grain of the tree
In Lettina's palm, the flesh frozen as the lapping
Of the sea stopped in wood.

And in the forest, he can put his hand on the trunk
Of the tree and feel how it shudders
In exactly the same way the sea trembles
Beneath a quivering figurehead, in the same way
Lettina grips the bedpost in the middle of the night
Whenever heavy clouds, like great whales, pass by,
Sounding in the dark.

It is one and the same sinking
That exists in the figurehead plunging
Between cold stormy waves and in the tree
Falling between icy crests of winter light
And in Lettina descending into the cold
Drowning of her dreams.

In the core of the tree Kioka has found

The two wooden crosses the figurehead holds
Toward the sky as she races over the seas
Into the center of the still forest, into the crux
Of Lettina's name. Only Kioka sees how a wooden
Figurehead and a single tree in the forest and Lettina
Can rise together as one, facing straight-on the direction
From which their only motion proceeds.

Before her visit comes to an end, Cecil
Wants to paint a portrait of Lettina, depicting
A detailed chronology of the metamorphosis
Of the tree from seed to flower or vice versa,
Illustrating simultaneously the history
Of female figureheads on clipper ships and the evolving
Essence of Lettina's soul, but no one (Kioka never truly
Understands the meaning of the question) will tell him
Where to begin.

Kioka rides his brown spotted pinto with naked boys
On naked ponies. They were his darlings
From the beginning, his darlings. Their stomachs
Pressed to the ponies' warm backs, their bare
Heels kicking, every one of them rides fast
With both hands free. Nothing will stop them.
They have the whole wide flat prairie of flowering bluet
Before the house, and they have the whole wide shining
Shore of sand before the sea.

Sonia, Gordon and Albert hurry to the second-story
Veranda to watch the naked boys on their ponies
Whenever they gallop past.

Gordon is pleased to discover that the dark
Blind column of the porch where he places his hand
For a moment contains all the knowledge anyone could pursue
Concerning the galloping hooves of ponies bounding
Over a blue prairie with naked boys on their backs.

Even though Felicia is asleep on a distant hillside
And cannot see or hear the ponies, still it is Kioka
Riding with naked boys who makes the only wide prairie
Of Felicia's heart. It is Kioka who gallops without stopping
Along the only wide shining shore of her heart.

Sonia wants to bring the blind beggars
To the second-story veranda when the ponies pass
So that they may watch the wind coming
Through those flower-filled manes to blow
Against their faces, so that they can see, thereby,
The course of their only cure. And she wants the deaf
Beggars to come and grip the prairie-filled porch railing
During that passing so that they may hear

The only method of their healing.

As the ponies pass, Albert, having removed
All his clothes, stands with his eyes closed
And his ears stopped and grips the column
Of the porch as he rises simultaneously and leaves
The second-story veranda to gallop past himself
On a wild pinto pony following Kioka toward the sea.

Cecil has climbed to the highest garret of the house
So that he can see how Kioka and his ponies reach the bay,
How nothing on the sky or the shore hesitates
As they continue straight out over the water, galloping
Across the waves, through the light-filled spray,
Their hooves striking hard against the flat sun on the surface
Of the sea, how they ride high above the deep, becoming
A rearing surging line of ocean rim racing along the sky.
He leans forward watching them into the evening, watching
Until they pass so far out of sight that he can hear them clearly,
Screaming and thundering and roaring at his back.

from

*Splitting and Binding*

## The Next Story

All morning long
they kept coming back, the jays,
five of them, blue-grey, purple-banded,
strident, disruptive. They screamed
with their whole bodies from the branches
of the pine, tipped forward, heads
toward earth, and swept across the lawn
into the oleanders, dipping low
as they flew over the half-skull
and beak, the blood-end of the one wing
lying intact, over the fluff
of feathers scattered and drifting
occasionally, easily as dandelion—
all that the cat had left.

Back and forth, past one another,
pausing as if listening, then sharply
cutting the morning again into shard
upon shard of frantic and crested descent,
jagged slivers of raucous outrage,
they kept at it, crying singly, together,
alternately, as if on cue, discordant
anthem. The pattern of their inconsolable
fear could be seen against the flat
spring sky as identical to the pattern
made by the unmendable shatter
of disjointed rubbish on the lawn,
*all morning long.*

Mothers, fathers, our kind, tell me again
that death doesn't matter. Tell me
it's just a limitation of vision, a fold
of landscape, a deep flax-and-poppy-filled
gully hidden on the hill, a pleat

in our perception, a somersault of existence,
natural, even beneficent, even a gift,
the only key to the red-lacquered door
at the end of the hall, "water
within water," those old stories.

But this time, whatever is said,
when it's said, will have to be more
reverent and more rude, more absolute,
more convincing then these five jays
who have become the five wheeling spokes
and stays of perfect lament, who, without knowing
anything, have accurately matched the black
beaks and spread shoulders of their bodies
to all the shrill, bird-shaped histories
of grief; will have to be demanding enough,
subtle enough, shocking enough, sovereign
enough, right enough to rouse me, to move me
from this window where I have pressed
my forehead hard against the unyielding pane,
unyielding all morning long.

## The Dead Never Fight Against Anything

It's always been that way.
They've allowed themselves to be placed,
knees to chin, in the corners of caves
or in holes in the earth, then covered
with stones; they've let their fingers
be curled around old spears or diadems
or favorite dolls, the stems
of cut flowers.

Whether their skulls were cracked open
and their brains eaten by kin
or whether their brains were pulled
by tongs through their nostrils
and thrown into the dog's dish as waste
are matters that have never concerned them.

They have never offered resistance
to being tied to rocks below the sea,
left for days and nights until their flesh
washed away or likewise to being placed
high in jungle trees or high on scaffolds
alone in the desert until buzzards,
vultures and harpy eagles stripped
their bones bare. They have never minded
jackals nosing at their haunches,
coyotes gnawing at their breasts.

The dead have always been so purely
tolerant. They've let their bones
be rubbed with ointments, ornamented
with ochre, used as kitchen ladles
and spoons. They've been imperturbably
indifferent to the removal of all
their entrails, the resulting cavities

filled with palm wine, aromatic
spices; they have lain complacently
as their abdomens were infused
by syringe with cedar oil.
They've allowed all seven
natural openings of their bodies
to be closed with gold dust.

They've been shrunken and their mouths
sewn shut; they've been wrapped
in gummed linen, corded, bound upright
facing east, hung above coals
and smoked, their ears stuffed
with onions, sent to sea on flaming
pyres. Not one has ever given
a single sign of dissent.

Oblivious to abuse. Even today,
you can hit them and pinch them
and kick them. You can shake them,
scream into their ears. You can cry.
You can kiss them and whisper and moan,
smooth their combed and parted hair, touch
the lips that yesterday spoke, beseech,
entreat with your finest entreaty.
Still, they stare without deviation,
straight into distance and direction.
Old stumps, old shameless logs, rigid
knurls, snow-faced, pitiless,
pitiless betrayal.

## The Voice of the Precambrian Sea

During the dearth and lack of those two thousand
Million years of death, one wished primarily
Just to grasp tightly, to compose, to circle,
To link and fasten skillfully, as one
Crusty grey bryozoan builds upon another,
To be *anything* particular, flexing and releasing
In controlled spasms, to make boundaries—replicating
Chains, membranes, epitheliums—to latch on with power
As hooked mussels now adhere to rocky beaches;
To roll up tightly, fistlike, as a water possum,
Spine and skin, curls against the cold;
To become godlike with transformation.

And in that time one eventually wished,
With the dull swell and fall of the surf, to rise up
Out of oneself, to move straight into the violet
Billowing of evening as a willed structure of flight
Trailing feet, or by six pins to balance
Above the shore on a swollen blue lupine, tender,
Almost sore with sap, to shimmer there,
Specific and alone, two yellow wings
Like splinters of morning.

One yearned simultaneously to be invisible,
In the way the oak toad is invisible among
The ashy debris of the scrub-forest floor;
To be grandiose as deserts are grandiose
With punctata and peccaries, Joshua tree,
Saguaro and the mule-ears blossom; to be precise
As the long gleaming hairs of the gourami, swaying
And touching, find the moss and roughage
Of the pond bottom with precision; to stitch
And stitch (that dream) slowly and exactly
As a woman at her tapestry with needle and thread

Sews each succeeding canopy of the rain forest
And with silver threads creates at last
The shining eyes of the capuchins huddled
Among the black leaves of the upper branches.

One longed to be able to taste the salt
Of pity, to hold by bones the stone of grief,
To take in by acknowledgment the light
Of spring lilies in a purple vase, five white
Birds flying before a thunderhead, to become
Infinite by reflection, announcing out loud
In one's own language, by one's own voice,
The fabrication of these desires, this day
Of their recitation.

# The Origin of Order

Stellar dust has settled.
It is green underwater now in the leaves
Of the yellow crowfoot. Its potentialities
Are gathered together under pine litter
As emerging flower of the pink arbutus.
It has gained the power to make itself again
In the bone-filled egg of osprey and teal.

One could say this toothpick grasshopper
Is a cloud of decayed nebula congealed and perching
On his female mating. The tortoise beetle,
Leaving the stripped veins of morning-glory vines
Like licked bones, is a straw-colored swirl
Of clever gases.

At this moment there are dead stars seeing
Themselves as marsh and forest in the eyes
Of muskrat and shrew, disintegrated suns
Making songs all night long in the throats
Of crawfish frogs, in the rubbings and gratings
Of the red-legged locust. There are spirits of orbiting
Rock in the shells of pointed winkles
And apple snails, ghosts of extinct comets caught
In the leap of darting hare and bobcat, revolutions
Of rushing stone contained in the sound of these words.

Maybe the paths of the Pleiades and Coma clusters
Have been compelled to mathematics by the mind
Contemplating the nature of itself
In the motions of stars. The pattern
Of the starry summer night might be identical
To the structure of the summer heavens circling
Inside the skull. I can feel time speeding now
In all directions deeper and deeper into the black oblivion

Of the electrons directly behind my eyes.

Child of the sky, ancestor of the sky, the mind
Has been obligated from the beginning
To create an ordered universe
As the only possible proof
Of its own inheritance.

## The Answering of Prayers

Because they have neither tongue
Nor voice, the iris are thought by some
Never to pray, also because they have no hands
To press together and because, born blind,
They cannot properly direct their eyes
Heavenward and, not insignificantly,
Because their god has no ears.

Rising simply from the cement
Of their bulbs, the iris have no premeditated
Motion. They never place one appendage
Deliberately before another in a series
Crossing space. How can they ever formulate, then,
A progress of thought moving from "want"
To "request," from "delight" to "blessing"?
How can they invent what they cannot envision—
A structure of steps leading from "self"
To "beyond"?

Consequently, and some may call it prayer,
They engage themselves in one steady proclamation
Which eventually becomes arched and violet
With petals, pertinently stemmed, budded
With nuance, a subtlety of lissome blades, a sound
Undoubtedly recognized by that deaf god
Who contains within his breast, like the sky-half
Of a spring afternoon, vacancies shaped
As missing floral clusters, purple-streaked
Intimacies. As rooted in his place as April,
It is their god who, standing hollow, precedes them
With the absence of brown-wine and lavender bouquets,
Ivory flags on grey-green stalks.

And in the unfolding act of his being filled,

As he becomes weighted, suffused with blossoms
And fragrance, as he feels his heart cupped
And pressed with the intensity of ascent,
In that act of being filled (perfect
Absolution) doesn't he surround, doesn't
He enable, doesn't he with fitting eloquence
Reply?

### The Importance of the Whale in the Field of Iris

They would be difficult to tell apart, except
That one of them sails as a single body of flowing
Grey-violet and purple-brown flashes of sun, in and out
Across the steady sky. And one of them brushes
Its ruffled flukes and wrinkled sepals constantly
Against the salt-smooth skin of the other as it swims past,
And one of them possesses a radiant indigo moment
Deep beneath its lidded crux into which the curious
Might stare.

In the early morning sun, however, both are equally
Colored and silently sung in orange. And both gather
And promote white prairie gulls which call
And circle and soar about them, diving occasionally
To nip the microscopic snails from their brows.
And both intuitively perceive the patterns
Of webs and courseways, the identical blue-glass
Hairs of connective spiders and blood
Laced across their crystal skin.

If someone may assume that the iris at midnight sways
And bends, attempting to focus the North Star
Exactly at the blue-tinged center of its pale stem,
Then someone may also imagine how the whale rolls
And turns, straining to align inside its narrow eye
At midnight, the bright star-point of Polaris.

And doesn't the iris, by its memory of whale,
Straighten its bladed leaves like rows of baleen
Open in the sun? And doesn't the whale, rising
To the surface, breathe by the cupped space
Of the iris it remembers inside its breast?

If they hadn't been found naturally together,

Who would ever have thought to say: The lunge
Of the breaching whale is the fragile dream
Of the spring iris at dawn; the root of the iris
Is the whale's hard wish for careful hands finding
The earth on their own?

It is only by this juxtaposition we can know
That someone exceptional, in a moment of abandon,
Pressing fresh iris to his face in the dark,
Has taken the whale completely into his heart;
That someone of abandon, in an exceptional moment,
Sitting astride the whale's great sounding spine,
Has been taken down into the quiet heart
Of the iris; that someone imagining a field
Completely abandoned by iris and whale can then see
The absence of an exceptional backbone arching
In purple through dark flowers against the evening sky,
Can see how that union of certainty which only exists
By the heart within the whale within the flower rising
Within the breaching heart within the heart centered
Within the star-point of the field's only buoyant heart
Is so clearly and tragically missing there.

*For the Wren Trapped in a Cathedral*

She can never remember how she entered—
What door, what invisible gate, what mistaken
Passage. But in this place every day,
The day shines as a muted mosaic of impenetrable
Colors, and during the black moonless nights,
Every flickering star lifts smoke, drips wax.
She flies, back and forth through the nave, small,
Bewildered among the forest of branchless trees,
Their straight stone trunks disappearing majestically
Into the high arches of the seasonless stone sky.
No weather here, except the predictable weather
Of chant and procession; no storm, except the storm
Of the watchdogs let loose inside at night.

Now when she perches on the bishop's throne
Her song naturally imitates the pattern
Of frills and flutes found in the carvings there,
The hanging fruit, profuse foliage, ripened
Curves. Her trills have adapted themselves
To fit perfectly the detailed abundance
Of that wooden Paradise.

And she has come to believe in gods, swerving close
To the brightness of the apse, attempting to match
Her spread wings, her attitude, to that of the shining
Dove caught there in poised flight above the Ark.
Near the window of the upper chapel, she imagines
She is that other bird, emanating golden rays
To the Christ in the river below.

Resting on a colonnade opposite the south wall
Of stained glass, she watches how the lines
Of her wings become scarlet and purple
With Mary's Grief. And when she flies the entire

Length of the side aisles, she passes
Through the brown-orange swath of light
From the Journey into Egypt, the green and azure
Of the Miracle of the Five Thousand Fed.
Occasionally she finds that particular moment
And place where she is magnificently transformed,
The dull brown of her breast becoming violet
And magenta with the Adoration of the Magi.

What is it that happens to her body, to bone
And feather and eye, when, on some dark evenings,
She actually sees herself covered, bathed, suffused
In the red blood of the Crucifixion?

Among the statues at night, she finds it a peace,
A serenity, to pause, to murmur in sleep
Next to the ear of a saint, to waken
Nested on the outstretched hand
Of the Savior's unchanging blessing.

Certainly she dreams often of escape, of reversing
That process by which she came to be here, leaving
As an ordinary emissary carrying her own story,
Sacred news from the reality of artifice,
Out into the brilliant white mystery
Of the truthful world.

## The Grooming

*Though your sins be as scarlet,*
*they shall become as white as snow.*

Isaiah I:18

Under the branches of the elm
and the tall, blooming bushes of black haw,
in the wavering jigsaw of the sun,
you sit, naked on the bench, waiting.
The paraphernalia is gathered,
laid out—warm wash water in a stainless-
steel bowl, rinse water in the deeper
pail, creams, soaps, a sanctuary
of flannel and towels.

She begins, holding each foot
in turn on her lap, carefully,
as if it were a basket of sweet fruits.
Her fingers stroke, wetting, soaping.
She washes the toes, the tender part
of the sole, over the swivel
of the ankle, the swell of the calf.

A hedge of slender sassafras
beside the road sways, almost female
in its graces, as you stand and turn
and she sponges behind your knees,
around each leg (they *are* pillars),
along the inner thighs, without rushing,
to the groin, the slick soap lathered
beneath her hand, the rag dipped
and wrung in rinse water.

She bathes the buttocks next,
and to the front, your genitals,
slowly, carefully. The sassafras sway,

and off in the distance, out of the center
of the rice field, a ceremony of sparrows
appears, releases, dissolves.

Up the strict hollow of the spine,
your torso, your neck, the clean water,
ladled and poured through the disciplined
light of the afternoon, finds its way
back down from your shoulders, following
every wrinkle and bead of nipple
and joint, like rain through leaves
and blossoms of yellow poplar, into the creases
of your sex and out again.

This is the form of absolution:
your hands in her attentive hands,
your arms inside her ministrations.

Listen . . . *elbow, your elbow.*

Can't you hear, in the sound
of its name, how it has been innocent
forever? And doesn't the entire body, touched
with honor, become honorable? Doesn't the body,
so esteemed and cherished, become
the place of divinity?

The face, the hair, laved,
toweled, rubbed, perfumed,
clean, radiant—you are new,
new as high-mountain snow
not even yet seen, snow so fine,
so weightless, so pervasive, it is one
with the white explosions of the wind,
one with the tight, steady bursting
of the moon, one with the hardest

and safest seams of the night,
by which you now know and so must declare:
the soul can never be more
than what the body believes
of itself.

## There Is a Way to Walk on Water

Over the elusive, blue salt-surface easily,
Barefoot, and without surprise—there is a way
To walk far above the tops of volcanic
Scarps and mantle rocks, towering seamounts
Rising in peaks and rifts from the ocean floor,
Over the deep black flow of that distant
Bottom as if one walked studiously
And gracefully on a wire of time
Above eternal night, never touching
Fossil reef corals or the shells of leatherbacks,
Naked gobies or the crusts of sea urchins.

There is a way to walk on water,
And it has something to do with the feel
Of the silken waves sliding continuously
And carefully against the inner arches
Of the feet; and something to do
With what the empty hands, open above
The weed-blown current and chasm
Of that possible fall, hold to tightly;
Something to do with how clearly
And simply one can imagine a silver scatter
Of migrating petrels flying through the body
During that instant, gliding with their white
Wings spread through the cartilage of throat
And breast, across the vast dome of the skull,
How distinctly one can hear them calling singly
And together inside the lungs, sailing straight
Through the spine as if they themselves believed
That bone and moment were passageways
Of equal accessibility.

Buoyant and inconsequential, as serious,
As exact as stone, that old motion of the body,

That visible stride of the soul, when the measured
Placing of each toe, the perfect justice
Of the feet, seems a sublimity of event,
A spatial exaltation—to be able to walk
Over water like that has something to do
With the way, like a rain-filled wind coming
Again to dry grasses on a prairie, all
Of these possibilities are remembered at once,
And the way, like many small blind mouths
Taking drink in their dark sleep,
All of these powers are discovered,
Complete and accomplished
And present from the beginning.

## Knot

Watching the close forest this afternoon
and the riverland beyond, I delineate
quail down from the dandelion's shiver
from the blowzy silver of the cobweb
in which both are tangled. I am skillful
at tracing the white egret within the white
branches of the dead willow where it roosts
and at separating the heron's graceful neck
from the leaning stems of the blue-green
lilies surrounding. I know how to unravel
sawgrasses knitted to iris leaves knitted
to sweet vernals. I can unwind sunlight
from the switches of the water in the slough
and divide the grey sumac's hazy hedge
from the hazy grey of the sky, the red vein
of the hibiscus from its red blossom.

All afternoon I part, I isolate, I untie,
I undo, while all the while the oak
shadows, easing forward, slowly ensnare me,
and the calls of the wood peewees catch
and latch in my gestures, and the spicebush
swallowtails weave their attachments
into my attitude, and the damp sedge
fragrances hook and secure, and the swaying
Spanish mosses loop my coming sleep,
and I am marsh-shackled, forest-twined,
even as the new stars, showing now
through the night-spaces of the sweet gum
and beech, squeeze into the dark
bone of my breast, take their perfectly
secured stitches up and down, pull
all of their thousand threads tight
and fasten, fasten.

## The Family Is All There Is

Think of those old, enduring connections
found in all flesh—the channeling
wires and threads, vacuoles, granules,
plasma and pods, purple veins, ascending
boles and coral sapwood (sugar-
and light-filled), those common ligaments,
filaments, fibers and canals.

Seminal to all kin also is the open
mouth—in heart urchin and octopus belly,
in catfish, moonfish, forest lily,
and rugosa rose, in thirsty magpie,
wailing cat cub, barker, yodeler,
yawning coati.

And there is a pervasive clasping
common to the clan—the hard nails
of lichen and ivy sucker
on the church wall, the bean tendril
and the taproot, the bolted coupling
of crane flies, the hold of the shearwater
on its morning squid, guanine
to cytosine, adenine to thymine,
fingers around fingers, the grip
of the voice on presence, the grasp
of the self on place.

Remember the same hair on pygmy
dormouse and yellow-necked caterpillar,
covering red baboon, thistle seed
and willow herb? Remember the similar
snorts of warthog, walrus, male moose
and sumo wrestler? Remember the familiar
whinny and shimmer found in river birches,

bay mares and bullfrog tadpoles,
in children playing at shoulder tag
on a summer lawn?

The family—weavers, reachers, winders
and connivers, pumpers, runners, air
and bubble riders, rock-sitters, wave-gliders,
wire-wobblers, soothers, flagellators—all
brothers, sisters, all there is.

Name something else.

## Rolling Naked in the Morning Dew

Out among the wet grasses and wild barley-covered
Meadows, backside, frontside, through the white clover
And feather peabush, over spongy tussocks
And shaggy-mane mushrooms, the abandoned nests
Of larks and bobolinks, face to face
With vole trails, snail niches, jelly
Slug eggs; or in a stone-walled garden, level
With the stemmed bulbs of orange and scarlet tulips,
Cricket carcasses, the bent blossoms of sweet William,
Shoulder over shoulder, leg over leg, clear
To the ferny edge of the goldfish pond—some people
Believe in the rejuvenating powers of this act—naked
As a toad in the forest, belly and hips, thighs
And ankles drenched in the dew-filled gulches
Of oak leaves, in the soft fall beneath yellow birches,
All of the skin exposed directly to the *killy* cry
Of the king bird, the buzzing of grasshopper sparrows,
Those calls merging with the dawn-red mists
Of crimson steeplebush, entering the bare body then
Not merely through the ears but through the skin
Of every naked person willing every event and potentiality
Of a damp transforming dawn to enter.

Lillie Langtry practiced it, when weather permitted,
Lying down naked every morning in the dew,
With all of her beauty believing the single petal
Of her white skin could absorb and assume
That radiating purity of liquid and light.
And I admit to believing myself, without question,
In the magical powers of dew on the cheeks
And breasts of Lillie Langtry believing devotedly
In the magical powers of early morning dew on the skin
Of her body lolling in purple beds of bird's-foot violets,
Pink prairie mimosa. And I believe, without doubt,

In the mystery of the healing energy coming
From that wholehearted belief in the beneficent results
Of the good delights of the naked body rolling
And rolling through all the silked and sun-filled,
Dusky-winged, sheathed and sparkled, looped
And dizzied effluences of each dawn
Of the rolling earth.

Just consider how the mere idea of it alone
Has already caused me to sing and sing
This whole morning long.

## When At Night

Suppose all of you came in the dark,
each one, up to my bed while I was sleeping;

Suppose one of you took my hand
without waking me and touched my fingers,
moved your lips the length of each one, down
into the crotch with your tongue and up again,
slowly sucking the nipple of each knuckle
with your eyes closed;

Suppose two of you were at my head, the breath
of one in my ear like a bird/moth thuddering
at a silk screen; the other fully engaged, mouth
tasting of sweetmeats and liquors,
kissing my mouth;

Suppose another drew the covers
down to my feet, slipped the loops
from the buttons, spread my gown,
ministering mouth again around the dark
of each breast, pulling and puckering
in the way that water in a stir
pulls and puckers a fallen
bellflower into itself;

Two at my shoulders to ease
the gown away, take it down
past my waist and hips, over my ankles
to the end of the bed; one of you
is made to adore the belly; one of you
is obsessed with dampness; at my bent
knees now, another watching, at my parted
thighs another; and one to oversee
the separation and one to guard the joining

and one to equal my trembling and one
to protect my moaning;

And at dawn, if everything were put
in place again, closing, sealing, my legs
together, straight, the quilt folded
and tucked to my chin; if all of you
stepped back, away, into your places,
into the translucence of glass
at the window, into the ground breezes
swelling the limber grasses, into the river
of insect rubbings below the field and the light
expanding the empty spaces of the elm, back
into the rising black of the hawk deepening
the shallow sky, and we all woke then
so much happier than before, well,
there wouldn't be anything
wrong in that, would there?

## *For Passions Denied: Pineywoods Lily*

Who knows what unrelieved yearning
finally produced the pink-and-lavender-wax control
of these petals, what continual longing
resulted in the sharp arcing of the leaves,
what unceasing obsession became itself
in the steady siren of the ruby stigma? That tense
line of magenta disappearing over the boundaries
of the blossom is so unequivocal in the decision
of its direction, one is afraid to look too long.

I can understand, perhaps, having a hopeless
passion for gliding beneath the sea, wanting to swim
leisurely, without breath, through green salt
and sun-tiered water, to sleep all night, lost
and floating among the stroking of the angelfish,
the weaving rags of the rays. And I can understand
an impossible craving to fly unencumbered,
without effort, naked and easily over sandstone
canyons, through the high rain of river-filled
gorges, to feel the passing pressures of an evening
sky against the forehead, against the breast.
And I can understand the desire to touch a body
that may never be touched, the frenzy to move
one's hand along a thigh into a darkness
which will never have proximity, to take into oneself
the entire perfume, the whole yeast and vibration
and seethe of that which will always remain
aloof, a desire so unrelenting it might easily turn
any blood or pistil at its deepest crux
to majestic purple.

I don't know what it is that a pineywoods lily,
with all her being, might wish for. Yet whatever dearest
thing this lily was denied, it's clear

she must very greatly have suffered, to be before us now
so striking in her bearing, so fearsome
in her rage.

## When You Watch Us Sleeping

When you see us lying scented
in our nightclothes, the patchwork
quilt wadded at our feet, coverlet
kicked aside, when you see us still
at midnight, our bare arms covered
with the moon-shadows of the hemlock
by the window, our hands latent
and half-open on the pillows by our heads;

When you come upon any of us buried
but breathing, close to the earth,
motionless as oak leaves beneath drifts
of oak leaves or curled inside silk
body-vases hanging from greasewood
and vetch or sprawled, languid
under the broad branches
of the baobab in summer heat,
when you hear us humming hoarsely
sometimes, scarcely wheezing, murmuring
like white hens at their roost;

When you watch the green anole
on the banyan, cool and slender
as a pod, the onyx grain of his eye
closed deep in green sunlight,
when you can see how he obviously
possesses in his body, even in the slack
scaly skin of rose beneath his jaw,
even in the posing net of his ribs,
even in the corpuscle of blood
at the tip of his tail,
how he possesses in his body alone
all the power he needs to rise
and declare, not merely truth,

but rapture;

The living body asleep, so great
a sum of beauty that a billion
zeroes follow it, the eyes
sealing the head so tightly
during those moments
that the infinity of possible
heavens inside can be clearly
perceived by anyone;
when you watch us sleeping,
when you see the purest
architecture of the ear,
the explicit faith of the knee,
the old guiltless unforgiving adoring
sweet momentary tremble of claim
in the breast . . .

Aren't you sorry?
Don't you love us?

## The Objects of Immortality

If I could bestow immortality,
I'd do it liberally—on the aim of the hummingbird,
The sea nettle and the dispersing skeletons of cottonweed
In the wind, on the night heron hatchling and the night heron
Still bound in the blue-green darkness of its egg,
On the thrice-banded crab spider and on every low shrub
And tall teasel stem of its most perfect places.

I would ask that the turquoise skimmer, hovering
Over backwater moss, stay forever, without faltering,
Without disappearing, head half-eaten on the mud, one wing
Under pine rubbish, one floating downstream, nudged
And spit away by foraging darters.

And for that determination to survive,
Evident as the vibration of the manta ray beneath sand,
As the tight concentration of each trout-lily petal
On its stem, as the barbed body curled in the brain
Of the burrowing echidna, for that intensity
Which is not simply the part of the bittern's gold eye
Most easily identified and remembered but the entire
Bittern itself, for that bird-shaped realization
Of effective pressure against oblivion, I would make
My own eternal assertion: Let that pressure endure.

And maybe this immortality can come to pass
Because continuous life, even granted to every firefly
And firebeetle and fireworm on earth, to the glowing clouds
Of every deep-sea squirt, to all electric eels, phosphorescent
Fishes and scaly, bright-bulbed extensions of the black
Ocean bottoms, to all luminous fungi and all torch-carrying
Creatures, to the lost light and reflective rock
Of every star in the summer sky, everlasting life,
Even granted to all of these multiplied a million times,

Could scarcely perturb or bother anyone truly understanding
The needs of infinity.

## On Being Eaten Alive

You know the most terrifying ways—giant fish,
reticulate python, saber-toothed cat,
army ants by the hundreds, piranha
by the scores. One can imagine
being scarlet in the blood
of a lion or rolled as pellets
in a wolf's belly or ossified
in the barreled bones
of a grizzly bear.

There are those who have been snatched
away without leaving a trace
into the flames (efficient bowels)
of a pine forest on fire or a burning
barn in August and those
who have been taken on rough tongues
of salt, smothered and lost
in a cavern full of sea.

I have seen others disappear
without a cry, wholly ingested,
limbs and hair and voice,
swallowed up irretrievably
by the expanding sac
of insanity.

But I like to think
of that old way, the most common
and slowest, the body disassembled,
diffused, slowly, consumed—particle
by particle, stigma, gradually, by stigma,
cell by cell—converted carefully, transfigured,
transformed, becoming finally both
a passing grain of blue above an early

evening silhouette of oaks and an inflation
of sun in low October fog, both the sigh
of bladed wind in beach grasses
and the sound of singing in the wings
of desert bats, becoming as close
to itself as the smooth night skin
lining the skull, as the white moaning
conch of its own hearing, the body
becoming gradually and remarkably
so indisputably so.

## Before I Wake

The turning of the marsh marigold coming slowly
Into its emergent bloom underwater; the turning
Of the coral sands over themselves and over their dunes
And over the scratchings of the scarab beetles
Turning over the dung of the desert doe; the pivoting
Of the eye of the bluefish turning inside the drawing light
Of its multiple school shifting its constellation
In the dark sea; this is the prayer of sleep
In which I lay myself down to dream.

The quiet enclosed by the burrowing wolf spider
Dragging its egg sac to the surface to sun;
The stillness covered by the barren strawberry
Making its fleshless seed on the rocky hill;
The study in the desert mushroom knotting itself
In the arid heat; the silence of the fetal sea horses
Bound in the pouch of their father; this is the dream
Of the soul in which I lay myself down to pray.

And I've asked the outward motion of the hollow web
Of the elm making leaf, and I've asked the inward motion
Of every glinting fin making the focus of the carp,
And I've asked the involution of the egg buds carried
In the dark inside the cowbirds circling overhead,
And I've asked the tight coiling and breaking
Of light traveling in the beads of the sawgrass
And the net of the sea oats splitting and binding
And splitting again over and over across the open lands
To keep me in this dream tonight through one prayer more.

from

*Geocentric*

# A Common Sight

There is at least one eye
for everything here this afternoon.
The algae and the yeasts, invisible
to some, for instance, are seen
by the protozoa; and the black-tailed
seeds of tadpoles are recognized
on sight by the giant, egg-carrying
water beetle. Brook trout have eyes
for caddisfly larvae, pickerel
for dragonfly nymphs; redfin shiners
bear witness to the presence
of flocks of water fleas.

The grains of the goldenrod
are valued, sought out, found
by the red-legged grasshopper who is,
in turn, noticed immediately
by the short-tailed shrew whose least
flitter alarms and attracts
the rodent-scoped eye
of the white-winged hawk.

There is an eye for everything.
The two-lined salamander watches
for the horsehair worm, as the stilt spider
pays sharp attention to midge fly,
crane fly. The cricket frog
will not pass unnoticed, being spied
specifically by the ringed raccoon,
and, despite the night beneath
the field, the earthworm, the grub
and the leafhopper larva are perceived
by the star-nosed mole.

So odd, that nothing goes unnoticed.
Even time has its testimony,
each copepod in the colony possessing
a red eyespot sensitive to the hour,
the entire congregation rising
as one body at dusk to touch the dark
where it exists above the pond.

And I have an eye myself
for this particular vision, this continuous
validation-by-sight that's given
and taken over and over by clam shrimp,
marsh treader, bobcat, the clover-coveting
honeybee, by diving teal, the thousand-eyed
bot fly, the wild and vigilant,
shadow-seeking mollusk mya.

Watch now, for my sake, how I stalk. Watch
how I secure this vision. Watch how long
and lovingly, watch
how I feed.

## In Addition to Faith, Hope and Charity

I'm sure there's a god
in favor of drums. Consider
their pervasiveness—the thump,
thump and slide of waves
on a stretched hide of beach,
the rising beat and slap
of their crests against shore
baffles, the rapping of otters
cracking molluscs with stones,
woodpeckers beak-banging, the beaver's
whack of his tail-paddle, the ape
playing the bam of his own chest,
the million tickering rolls
of rain off the flat-leaves
and razor-rims of the forest.

And we know the noise
of our own inventions—snare and kettle,
bongo, conga, big bass, toy tin,
timbals, tambourine, tom-tom.

But the heart must be the most
pervasive drum of all. Imagine
hearing all together every tinny
snare of every heartbeat
in every jumping mouse and harvest
mouse, sagebrush vole and least
shrew living across the prairie;
and add to that cacophony the individual
staccato tickings inside all gnatcatchers,
kingbirds, kestrels, rock doves, pine
warblers crossing, criss-crossing
each other in the sky, the sound
of their beatings overlapping

with the singular hammerings
of the hearts of cougar, coyote,
weasel, badger, pronghorn, the ponderous
bass of the black bear; and on deserts too,
all the knackings, the flutterings
inside wart snakes, whiptails, racers
and sidewinders, earless lizards, cactus
owls; plus the clamors undersea, slow
booming in the breasts of beluga
and bowhead, uniform rappings
in a passing school of cod or bib,
the thidderings of bat rays and needlefish.

Imagine the earth carrying this continuous
din, this multifarious festival of pulsing
thuds, stutters and drummings, wheeling
on and on across the universe.

This must be proof of a power existing
somewhere definitely in favor
of such a racket.

# A Voice Speaks in Earnest, but Nobody Listens

Folly, I tell them, to build nests
of mosses, lichens, twigs and shredded
grape bark, even a deep, well-made cup
of grasshairs, cobwebs, plant fibers,
or a gourd-shaped, feather-lined cradle
of mud; folly to dig burrows in sandbanks,
among mesquite and prickly pear, to make
alleyways and warrens, to make dens in hummocks,
tussocks, weed clumps, dwarf willows.

Ridiculous, to home in hollow logs, I say,
to roost in cavern crevices, to attach
to sea fans, in eelgrass beds or rubble
bottoms, to wrap up in a sea whip or a vase
sponge, to seek kelp and algal holdfasts.

These barbels, pinchers, beaks, claws,
thorns, sticky stems, spikes and tusks—
absurd, futile—scent glands, ink bags,
twelve-tined antlers, long golden spines,
even beadlike spines in a ring.

Puffings, hissings, hindfeet thumpings,
barking coughs and bugling calls, warning
whistles, buzzes, yaps, pippings, *krees*,
*chicarees* and *cutta cutta cuttas*—vanity,
all vanity.

Pure folly, I repeat, to put forth lobes
and branchlets, heart-shaped petals, lavender
flowers in wet grassy meadows, bracts and bell-like
blossoms, pink berries, waxy drupes, winged
keys, seeded capsules by the scores.

So surrounded by dark, distant, flaring
combustions, histories and uncertainties,
it's a folly obviously, I tell them, to bring forth
blue-green eggs speckled with olive, white eggs
blotched with brown, black-spotted, clay-colored
eggs, pale eggs laid on sprigs of evergreen, womb
eggs, floating eggs, buried eggs, strings
of jelly eggs in slow riffles. A folly, I say,
to bring forth ever—stop, listen—to give
birth, to bear . . .

# That's Why

*Both the eye and the mind are*
*notoriously fallible instruments.*
**Stephen Jay Gould**

Can we trust then this scarlet banana flower
of the eye, shining in the lantern light,
or the dawn bat of the retina, seeming to cling there,
smaller than the blossom, taking, with her clean
mouse-tail tongue, nectar from the nectary?

Can the flighty mind be depended upon
rightly to detect the solid grasp
of her wiry nails, the hook of her long deformed
finger into the pod? Should the mind's eye
likewise be expected to see the invisible
tropical forest in the blackness beyond, the spicy
petai, the coveted fruit of the durian?

The bat's mind, we know, sees very well
by other than light. And we can be led
in the night without lantern to the right
blossom by the small heat of her beating heart
sensed even with both eyes closed.

Is it the eye's heart then or the mind's vision
that decides suddenly to call the blossom *mother?*
Is it the mind willed by the heart or the pure
eye alone that wants to name this silent supping
*spirit?* How can we know if it is merely
a blind heart's error or the mind's mad desire
to perfect itself or the eye through the eye
of the universe that sees *redemption*
as bat belly pressing hard to flower flesh
in a jungle night?

173

Senseless forest, special flower, sucking
beast, stay. In our certain fallibility,
be infallibly generous. Wait for us.

Indecent, self-soiled, bilious
reek of turnip and toadstool
decay, dribbling the black oil
of wilted succulents, the brown
fester of rotting orchids,
in plain view, that stain
of stinkhorn down your front,
that leaking roil of bracket
fungi down your back, you
purple-haired, grainy-fuzzed
smolder of refuse, fathering
fumes and boils and powdery
mildews, enduring the constant
interruption of sink-mire
flatulence, contagious
with ear wax, corn smut,
blister rust, backwash
and graveyard debris, rich
with manure bog and dry-rot
harboring not only egg-addled
garbage and wrinkled lip
of orange-peel mold but also
the clotted breath of overripe
radish and burnt leek, bearing
every dank, malodorous rut
and scarp, all sulphur fissures
and fetid hillside seepages, old,
*old*, dependable, engendering
forever the stench and stretch
and warm seethe of inevitable
putrefaction, nobody
loves you as I do.

## Teaching a Sea Turtle Suddenly Given the Power of Language, I Begin by Saying:

This green translucent continuance
through which you turn and function, rolling and twisting,
which fluctuates in darkness, which pulses and pushes
insistently against your forehead and your belly
and your genitals, to the top of which you must rise for light,
for breath, is called 'The Great Sea.'

And by these fingers, of which you have none, I am tracing
the curve of your horned beak, tracing your flippers
intricately scaled in canvas, moving down over the wooden
knobs of your back, down to the leather prick of your tail,
tracing all the boundaries of that which is called 'self,'
'Great Turtle of the Great Sea.'

And you must try to remember that heavy, ponderous,
slow-shifting silence which is everything you didn't know
you knew before your voice. Say 'silence' and listen.
Say 'silence.'

And your motion is called 'gliding, soaring
propulsion of self' and the passing, one after another,
of seaweed clusters and floating eels and rainbow wrasse
and scattered obelia is called 'time.' Say 'compelled,'
say 'driven,' say 'recognition of compulsion.'

Understand how you will eventually make the facts of the earth
by the hard drag-marks of your body over the dunes,
how by interference you will make the aggravated existence of
    bark
and grit and rut and sandbur. Say 'egg,' say 'begat,' say 'birth,
in the warm sandy loam.' Say 'birth by the nearest silver egg
buried in the sky.' Say 'invisible glass turtles pulling up
the black beaches above, leaving in the night

the scattered glow of their daring eggs.'
Say 'fancy.'

Here at the bottom of the sea, beneath the pock-marked
boulder, beside the extending and withdrawing feathers
of the polyps, in the definite turn and focus
of your reflective eye, here is where you must begin now
to be engaged in the making of your brain, each new word
bringing a salt-pulsing neuron simultaneously
into existence. Listen, I am telling you,
it is from the awareness of this precise moment
that the creation of yourself begins.

## Life and Death: All the Lost
## Accordions and Concertinas

You may wonder yourself what happened to them.
They're at the bottom of the sea.
Some people saw them floating downward,
discarded, sinking slowly into that foreign plane.

They were humming and chording
all the while, inside a confetti of bubbles,
their bellows expanding, opening
like the folded fins of butterfly fish.
Their leather straps were fluttering
behind them like ribbon fish, writhing
like eels, attached like lampreys.

A cargo of concertinas sailed
the salt surface momentarily, bobbing
like a fleet of air-filled jellyfish.

Down they all went, schools and cities
of them, turning and tumbling,
mother-of-pearl buttons gleaming,
keys and reeds quivering.

They recline there yet where they settled,
half-buried in muddy sand, tilting
on cliffs of coral, bobbled and nosed
by jacks and rays. Their bodies
teeter, bowing, contracting
to the tempo of the surf.
They wheeze and blow nightly
with the currents, singing like sirens,
shimmering in their treble, tenor treble.
Their sound is the same sound
you can imagine hearing if beds of waving

seaweed were a chorus of violins.

They take in and give forth their element.
They breathe and moan, those eternal
lungs. They speak. They are greater
than ghosts.

Their soliloquies circle the wide sea,
rippled and meditative, are heard
by nursing blue whales,
who answer.

## Diving for Gold: The Bottom of the World

*That which is far off and exceeding deep,*

*who can find it out?*

Ecclesiastes 7:24

Slipping down beneath thick shelves of ice,
into the green-blue shadows and planes,
the frigid, salt-smothers of the sea, your cords
and tubes and tanks, the mask, into the crude
currents that press against the limbs
and spine, that swing loose ties
and straps like a prairie wind;

it's worth it, even the shock
and cold-plastic rigidity of the fingers,
even the buffeting, even the freezing,
solidifying recitations and rules, the ice-crystal
constrictions of the breath; downward,
inward and down through the easy sluice
of the sea, into the slick swallow of the cold
sea, sinking so far and so deep that finally
the sound of *deep*, the pronunciation
of *deep*, the ringing of *deep*, recedes
and returns, circles and tides, involutes,
turns itself upside down, the head below
the feet now, the motion like rising
yet descending still, the voice of the self
heard resolutely from without now,
the hollow of the heart informing now
from both sides of the eyes;

the body a particle thus suspended
weightless at mid-heaven of the vast,
encompassing ocean; looking clearly, far,
farther into any direction than before,
you might discern what you foresaw

seeing—those million, faint campfires
of stars everywhere, their still threads
of smoke, the old, well-fed hunters
hunched beside them telling your story,
fiery constellations shining like grains
of gold along every crest and ridge
and creviced valley of the billowing,
black mountains extending above
and below, away and beyond.

# Good Heavens

## I

The common garden snail can't watch
the heavens and enumerate—600 young
stars in Perseus, one more hour
until full moon. It can't make lists—
pinwheel of Andromeda, comet fireball
of Tempel-Tuttle. It has never called
its slither the soft finger of night
nor its wound shell a frozen
galactic spin. Yet its boneless,
thumb-sized head is filled and totally
deaf with exactly the same tone
and timbre as the sky.

## II

*Winter Midnight*

It seemed I was looking into the face
of a vendor, skin so dark
I couldn't focus at first,
the stark structure of his skull
tighter, blacker even than his eyes.
It was a vendor with his wares—glass
bulbs and seeds, silver goats, loops
and strings of copper, brass-cathedral
charms, polished couples on sticks
copulating, twisted bracelets
and rings—spread like a market
of stars on the blanket at his knees.
I thought I saw borders, ways
and measures in his onyx face.

A shifty hawker, a familiar swindler,
it was an old, skinny vendor on folded
knees, kneeling purple bones, a skeleton
of vestments, a posture of spirals
and stocks hovering above and below
his spread of sockets and hoops,
reaching, rocking, merchandising
at my elbow: *Kum, laydee, bye,*
*kum bye mine.*

## III

To imagine stars and flaming
dust wheeling inside the gut
of a blind, transparent fish
swimming out-of-sight in the black
waters of a cave a thousand years ago
is to suggest that the perfect
mystery of time, motion and light
remains perfect.

## IV

Good—because the heavy burnings
and fumings of evolving
star clusters and extragalactic
cacophonies—because the flaming
Cygnus Loop, still whipping
and spewing sixty thousand years
after its explosion—because
the churning, disgorging womb
of the Great Nebula and the rushing
oblivions left from the collapse
of protostars—because suffocating

caverns of pulling, sucking gases
and pursuing, encircling ropes
of nuclear bombardments—
because erupting cauldrons
of double stars and multiple
stars flinging outward great
spires and towers of searing
poisons—because all of these
for this long have stayed
far, *far* away from our place.

## Elinor Frost's Marble-topped Kneading Table

Imagine that motion, the turning and pressing,
the constant folding and overlapping, the dough
swallowing and swallowing and swallowing itself
again, just as the sea, bellying up the hard shore,
draws back under its own next forward-moving
roll, slides out from under itself
along the beach and back again; that first
motion, I mean, like the initial act
of any ovum (falcon, leopard, crab) turning
into itself, taking all of its outside surfaces
inward; the same circular mixing and churning
and straightening out again seen at the core
of thunderheads born above deserts; that involution
ritualized inside amaryllis bulbs
and castor beans in May.

Regard those hands now, if you never
noticed before, flour-caked fists and palms knuckling
the lump, gathering, dividing, tucking
and rolling, smoothing, reversing. I know,
from the stirring and sinking habits
of your own passions, that you recognize
this motion.

And far in the distance, (you may even
have guessed) far past Orion and Magellan's vapors,
past the dark nebulae and the sifted rings
of interstellar dust, way beyond mass and propulsion,
before the first wheels and orbits of sleep
and awareness, there, inside that moment
which comes to be, when we remember,
at the only center where it has always been,
an aproned figure stands kneading, ripe
with yeast, her children at her skirts.

Now and then she pauses, bends quickly,
clangs open the door, tosses another stick
on the fire.

## Snow Thinking

Someone must have thought of snow falling first,
before it happened. That's what I believe,
someone way before me, way before anyone
could write "snow" and then see it happen—
in the cracks between the mud bricks
of the patio, assuming the shapes
of seeded sedum and wineleaf, covering
the tops of overturned flowerpots,
so much whiter than the sky it comes from—
as we do sometimes.

I think it must have come (the being
of the motion of snow, I mean, furling out
of the black, this method of winding
and loosening, this manner of arriving)
first from deep inside someone, as we say,
out of some quiet, exuberant graciousness,
far beyond neutron or electron, way before
eyes or hands, far before any crudeness
like that.

It had to come from someone first,
before snow, this expression of snow,
the swift, easy, multi-faceted
passion possessed and witnessed
in descending snow. It must be so.
Otherwise, how could we, as ourselves,
recognize it now—the event of snow,
so clearly eloquent, so separate,
so much rarer than snow? It's there.
We know it—the succumbing to sky,
the melding, nothing too small
for the embracing, a singular gentleness.

And don't we know now, without seeing it,
without touching it, that outside the window
the snow is coming, accumulating over the walls
and hedges of the garden, covering
the terra cotta, filling all the filigree
and deficiencies of evening?

I believe that snow snowing is the form
of someone singing in the future
to a new and beloved child, a child who,
staring up at the indistinguishable
features of his mother's star-filled face
in the dark, knows, without touching
or seeing, the experience of snow, opening
his mouth to catch and eat every spark
of the story as it breaks and falls
so particularly upon him.

# Distance and Depth

Whether looking down through
a pond's surface, past a brown mossy
tavern of twigs into a floating nest
and through the membrane of a single
translucent egg globule, down
into the drama and complex carnival
of that jelly mote, its lipids,
ashes and crystal inclusions,
through its loops and plots
and domestications, past bound
messages, gates, stringy messengers,
past storms, sparks, signs and orbits,
on down toward the tense purple
nebula of chaos at its core;

Or whether watching far out over
the flat grasses and gullies, skimming
the plains past low opuntia, hidden
beeflies, jumping mice, the burrows
of dogs and deer and all that multitude,
right up to the first rising red rock
range and past that to the next sheer
evergreen plateau and on beyond
to the ultimate highest blue snow
of the peaks with names, past them
to the ragged ridge of the sinking moon
and behind that into the easy black
where the eyes seem suddenly turned
hard and fast on themselves;

whether distance or depth, either way
it's evident there are fields and fields
and fields aplenty, more and more
space than is needed, ample space

for any kind of sin to be laid down,
disassembled, swallowed away, lost,
absorbed, forgotten, transformed,
if one should only ask
for such a favor.

## By Death

In that moment she became two, one sitting
among the red flags of the blackbirds
in the reeds, the other standing fixed
like a poplar in a fence of poplars.

In the next second, there were four
of her, one watching evening from the sill
beside the bed, another laced through the night-
spaces between the fireflies.

In a further splitting, she was eight,
and in the next sixteen, one blue
by paper lantern, one amethyst by evening
smoke, one ringed like ice by a winter
moon, one ringed like a lily-pond by rain,
one marked by murder, one veined
by acquittal.

And there were thirty-two of her then
and again sixty-four, and she was simultaneously
over a plain of summer cress and under
a reef of evening coral, within a knob
of shyster thistle, within a bud of thresher
shark, sailing by roots of bony fish,
soaring by fins of tamarack and phlox.

With the next turning she became
a hundred and twenty-eight of herself, groomed
the horse of Orion, dwelled in the light-remnant
of Vela. She was wind through the scaffold
of pity, a nesting owl among the eaves of praise.
Then two hundred fifty-six—she was stone as well,
and zephyr, then legion, then too various
to be reckoned, too pervasive to be noticed,
too specific to be named.

"In order to define the issue . . ." he begins,
as an orange one leaps from the piano, lands
in the middle of the room on the floral
carpet, bounds again, climbs half-way
up the silk drapes and stops, legs spread,
hanging as if suspended there.

"Time in a timeless . . ." she pauses,
as the calico jumps from her lap, scrambles
up the drapes, chasing the swishing
orange tail of the other.

A short-haired yellow one skids
around the corner, at this point, sliding,
skittering, batting at a rolling bell, jangling
and spinning it down the marble hallway.

"Heredity definitely plays
a role," he replies.

"It's a simple matter of give
and take," she responds, as a grey one falls
from the chandelier, lands on the head
of a tabby, slides off, raking
one ear with a hind claw (just a slight
suggestion of blood).

Two toms race through the open
door at this moment, thud along the couch, fly
from the top of the chintz armchair
to the mantelpiece, spilling a brass jar
of round rum candies.

"Even god as a concept . . ." he continues,

while an old matted white one sips perfumed
water from a vase of camellias
sitting on a buffet before the mirror.

"If we could just catch hold . . ."
she whispers. Three thin black ones,
sitting on the icy window sill outside, peer
into the parlour with indignant longing.

She sighs, stretches, slowly licks
her finger, wets and winds a neck curl
into place, while he watches,
swaying, hind quarters wriggling
until he pounces, catches and pulls loose
in a sudden release of one motion
the trailing sash of her cashmere robe.

# Under the Big Top

*. . . though I walk through*
*the valley of the shadow . . .*

Psalm 23

They're always here. One of them tumbles
in her maroon and silver-sequined tights before me,
as if she led, down the road. She somersaults, flips
mid-air over a hedge row, her bodice sparkling, over
a patch of butterfly pea. She does hand-stands
off curbs, cartwheels down alleys, leapfrogs
past parking meters. Crossing any bridge
with her is ceremony, a ritual of back bends
on thin wooden railings, toe-dances
on suspension cables.

How can I fear, one going ahead armed with chair
and fake pistol, two going ahead in epaulettes and brass
buttons, with marching drum, bold tasseled baton?

Another keeps a constant circle of blossoms
and pods spinning around my head. Tossing
and catching, he weaves almonds, apples, limes,
pomegranates, once the spotted eggs of the wood peewee,
once the buds of the Cherokee rose. So deft,
nothing he handles falls or shatters or bruises.
Even in the night far ahead I can see his torches,
their flames spiralling high into the black
dome, down again into his waiting hands.

And this one, such comfort, shuffles at my pace,
following one step behind. Holding his purple
pint-sized parasol above my head, he recovers
from each of his stumbles, tripping over stray dogs,
paper cups, raindrops, stepping on the dragging
cuffs of his own striped trousers. He keeps up,

guffawing when he hears me laugh, stopping abruptly
if I cease. And when he sees tears in my eyes,
he takes out his cowboy hankie, honks his schnoz,
presses two sad fingertips sincerely
to his garish grin.

Many saw them taken away, crowded
in the wagons, chained together,
their oblong white faces peering
through the slats, eyebrows arched high
with bewilderment. All those joeys,
some were wearing cup-sized black
bowlers on their bald heads,
others topless top hats
resting on their ears, orange neckties
down to their knees. A few
blew on bubble pipes and pondered
the sky as the wagons bumped along.
One in baggy blue coat, a tin foil
star pinned to his chest, beat
the others repeatedly
with his billy club balloon.

Their painted tears
looked real.

Later, after the last wagon
had disappeared into the mountains,
that was a bad time for all merchants
selling floppy chartreuse satin pajamas
with big ball buttons, tent-sized
trousers of tartan plaid and purple
stripes. The Squirting Plastic
Flower Company and the Six-Inch Bicycle
Factory had to close shop completely.
Fox terriers, trained to wear
bonnets and ride in baby buggies,
lost their jobs. Soon the youngest
children couldn't remember a shivaree,
the parade of stunts, midget cars

or prancing piglets, the "walk-around"
on the Hippodrome track.

Then toward the end of that year,
visionaries began to appear, the first one
claiming to have seen the stiltman at dusk
striding in his gold metallic suit
through a copse of slender prairie
poplars in the shadowy evening sun,
another swearing to have witnessed
Petrolino himself wearing his pointed
hat topped with bells, ducking down
and popping up among the swaying
cattails, frightening all the blackbirds
in the most comical way. A third, watching
a distant field of autumn milkweed,
testified to seeing confetti
fly into the air from the old
empty-water-bucket gag.
Even a grandmother living alone
heard Grimaldi singing "An Oyster
Crossed in Love" beneath the scraping
branches outside her window
just before dawn.

But on a windy evening at midnight,
when a whole party of laughing people
together saw one of their favorites
stumbling on the sidewalk in the bluster,
tripping up the curb, reeling
against a trash can, somersaulting
again headfirst, sprawling
and pitching, taking his pratfalls
down the street like a blowing tangle
of open newspaper, then no one dared
deny any longer the truths

of spirits and souls, that bold new
rumor of resurrection.

While all the seas harass themselves
with whipping waterspouts and typhoons,
while all the seas draw back
out of themselves into still poplar
prairies and sheaths of ice, while Lily,
her spine pressed against the oak, murders
her baby in the forest, and Hubert
at tea time hands Rose a lemon wedge
and cream—all along it continues
to move along, that wagon, its bed
planed and pegged like a floor,
its sides like a farm wagon
slatted and high.

Where the mottled mongrel, chained
to the shed, meets the returning howl
of his own barking at midnight,
where the spotted salamander
at the pond's edge relinquishes
its color and motion to the blooming
milfoil, where the eye of the snow hare,
alone on a white plain, becomes
the only true vortex and blizzard of winter,
there it passes also, creaking
and swaying, the hub of each wheel turning
like a coin spun on a table, each spoke
circling like a lighthouse beacon.

It passes the fallen and fern-cradling
tree from which it is constructed,
passes the ocean valley from which its lumber
will grow, passes the sleeping infant
who has forged its axle, passes the grave
of the smith who will ring its wheels,

passes blind Edith who points and shouts,
"See the flaming wagon crossing the sky,"
passes Uncle Morris reciting, "There lies
the wagon, broken, upside down in the ditch,"
passes itself, sides hung with orchis
and lavender, wheels laced with sage,
inside the visionary's mind.

It sways and rumbles, traveling always
both subsequent and prior to every moment
of its path. Don't you know it? Can't you see?
You, riding along with all of its passengers,
standing up, laughing now, waving
your hat, hallooing and hallooing?

## The Mad Linguist

It takes several scholars working together
to translate her orations. Even then
no one understands completely. Just listen
to the multiple tentacles and bivalve forms
in the language of this one, the constructions
winding like the whorls of a whelk's shell
around their axis. The trained ear can hear
the many small coordinated spider claws
of nuance there, a rapidity of staccato
syllables sounding like the sharp toes
of purple shore crabs scurrying over the sand.

And listen to the strangeness of this speech,
logic that progresses in a network
of ever-smaller branches spreading outward
as a poplar spreads clear to the thin
veins at the edges of its yellow leaves.
Here every verb contains a subtle allusion
to ascension; predicates rise vertically
out of pines into the sky.
What an ideal language for describing
the emotional state of anyone who feels
the recitations of seven thousand
riverside birches trembling in his bones.

She is equally at ease in the tongues
of temperature and sun, voicing the same slow,
careful vowels that barely sound in a warming
April field, the scrape and rasping whisper
of shifting stones being pushed aside
by the roots of partridge peas. She pronounces
each syllable with the quiverings found
in the buds of verbena, the throbbings
in the pods of the swallowtail.

Will the deaf and blind of spring,
who hear only by their armless, legless
bodies lying beneath the soft soil,
now be able to understand
her every assertion?

"All spoken words presuppose the existence
of an audience that perceives them," she quotes
from an ancient language that pauses
and plunges forward in leaps and lurches
like a prehistoric grizzly pouncing once
in the rushing snow-melt, pouncing again,
catching finally and lifting to the shore
the sweet flesh of the struggling silver fish
we know so well.

# The Process

First she gave all that she carried
in her arms, setting those trinkets down easily.
Then she removed her scarlet sash and gave it
for bandage, her scarf for blindfold, her shawl,
her handkerchief for shroud.

She let her violet kimono slip from her shoulders,
giving it too, because it was warm and could surround,
enwrap like dusk, and because it held her dark-river,
night-swimmer fragrances tight in the deep
stitches of its seams.

And she cut off her hair, offering its strands
for weaving, for pillow, lining, talisman,
for solace.

She gave her bracelets, the rings
from her fingers—those circles of gold jingling
like crickets, those loops of silver
chiming like spring—and gave her hands as well,
her fingers, the way they could particularize.

Her feet and their balance, her legs
and their stride, she relinquished;
and her belly, her thighs, her lap—wide, empty,
open as a prairie—her breasts full of sunlight,
like peaches and honey, like succor. She gave away
her bones—ribcage for scaffold, spine,
smaller knuckles for kindling, for sparks,
for flame.

And what remained—her face, her visage
reflective, transparent as sky—she gave
and even her word, her name, its echo,

until all, everything was given and everything
received, and she was no one,
gone, nothing,
god.

## The Greatest Grandeur

Some say it's in the reptilian dance
of the purple-tongued sand goanna,
for there the magnificent translation
of tenacity into bone and grace occurs.

And some declare it to be an expansive
desert—solid rust-orange rock
like dusk captured on earth in stone—
simply for the perfect contrast it provides
to the blue-grey ridge of rain
in the distant hills.

Some claim the harmonics of shifting
electron rings to be most rare and some
the complex motion of seven sandpipers
bisecting the arcs and pitches
of come and retreat over the mounting
hayfield.

Others, for grandeur, choose the terror
of lightning peals on prairies or the tall
collapsing cathedrals of stormy seas,
because there they feel dwarfed
and appropriately helpless; others select
the serenity of that ceiling/cellar
of stars they see at night on placid lakes,
because there they feel assured
and universally magnanimous.

But it is the dark emptiness contained
in every next moment that seems to me
the most singularly glorious gift,
that void which one is free to fill
with processions of men bearing burning

cedar knots or with parades of blue horses,
belled and ribboned and stepping sideways,
with tumbling white-faced mimes or companies
of black-robed choristers; to fill simply
with hammered silver teapots or kiln-dried
crockery, tangerine and almond custards,
polonaises, polkas, whittling sticks, wailing
walls; that space large enough to hold all
invented blasphemies and pieties, 10,000
definitions of god and more, never fully
filled, never.

New Poems

*Old Spiral of Conception*

## Till My Teeth Rattle

Why is it always arresting—
the sight of that same metal-sharp
disc of moon slicing slick and clean
as if it spun on a motor through
purple autumn clouds?

Likewise, I'm startled, taken aback
this morning, by three long-tailed
weasels humping cattywampus across
the gravel road, disappearing
into the weed-tunnels of oxeye daisy
and dock in the roadside ditches.

There's a whole prairie of popped
yucca pods, an overdone, unrestrained
confetti-spilling deluge of seeds
that's stopped me before, and I admit
I've stared—a tribe of darkling beetles
on the path, all standing on their heads,
black rear-ends to the wind. Like this,
like this, like this.

Whoever said *the ordinary, the mundane,
the commonplace?* Show them to me.

Wait a minute—a hummingbird moth
so deep now inside a rose petunia
that its petals flutter too, like wings.

There's no remedy, I suppose—this body
just made from the beginning to be shocked,
constantly surprised, perpetually stunned,
poked and prodded, shaken awake,
shaken again and again roughly, rudely,

then left, even more bewildered,
even more amazed.

## In My Time

It's easy to praise things present—the belligerent
stance of the woodhouse toad, the total
self-absorption of the frostweed blossom.
It's simple to compliment a familiar mess
of curly dock, the serene organization
of common onion reeds, the radish bulb
and its slender purple tail. And I like the way
the jay flings dirt furiously this morning
from the window box, the ridiculous shakings
of his black beak.

But it's not easy to praise things yet-to-come—
the nonexistent nubs of mountains not risen
from beneath the floor of the sea
or a new sound from some new creature,
descended maybe from our golden peepers
and white-chinned chuggers, that sound
becoming synonymous, for someone else,
with spring.

How can I appreciate light from an aging
sun shining through new configurations neither pine
nor ash? How can I extol the nurturing
fragrances from the spires, the spicules
of a landscape not yet formed or seeded?

I can praise these flowers today—the white yucca
with its immersing powder-covered moth, the desert
tahoka daisy and the buffalo gourd—but never
the future strangeness that may eventually
take their places.

From here now, I simply praise in advance
the one who will be there then,
so moved, as I, to do the praising.

## The Need to Adore

There is a need, a craving I have
to adore something as charitable
as the rambling scarlet sea fig, fruit
and blossom surfeiting the shore,
and something as certain as the undeviating
moon moving, like a gold marble
down a groove, exactly along its golden,
autumn corridor.

I have a passion to love something
as ministering as the morning penetrating
clear to the bottom of the pond, touching
the earth-side and sky-side of each leaf
of white water crowfoot, hornwort,
enclosing the blooming parsnip, petal-side,
stem-side, surrounding tadpole shrimp,
carp and cooter and mollusk, mud-side,
rock-side, to love something possessing
such lenient measures of inner
and outer circumference.

I know my hunger to worship something
as duplicitous as the peaceful aardwolf
and as fearsome as hounds on a fallen doe,
something as pliant and amenable as honeysuckle
vining a fence, as consummate as stone,
as fickle as jellyfish threads in a sea current,
to worship with abandon that which is as weak
as the neckbone of a button quail, fast
as fires on the Serengeti, silent
as the growth by grains of rock spires
in a damp cave, something that sails
in waves like needlegrasses across
the summer afternoon and something that falls

like fragrances of pine mold and mushroom
in forests filled with rain.

There is a need, my obsession, to submit
wholly, without reservation, to give entirely
to something lucent enough and strict enough,
fabled enough and fervent enough to encompass
all of these at once, something rudimentary
enough to let me enter, something
complete enough to let me go.

## Emissaries

How will we convince them,
when we return, of the beating crimson
of the honeycreeper's body, the quaking
violet rump of the velvet cuckoo wasp,
or simply of an easy night rain
over hills, that dizzy falling, grains
of moisture the size and multitude
of stars, a rain not lull and loop
alone but a perfect elucidation
of sleep? How can we describe it to them?

How will they understand the scaffold
of logic or the shape of mercy,
with neither the informing patterns
of the swallow's nest nor the radiating
structure of needles on a slash pine
in their memories to help them, without
even the razzling of poplar leaves
in an evening wind or the intensity
of spotted trout braced against clear
currents in their speech to help them?

How will they know how to perceive
without ever having witnessed
the grasping talents of the moon snail,
the salt-marsh snail?

Maybe they won't be able to attend
to us at all, not realizing how the sooty
owl attends, how the black-tailed jack
and the hoary cress and coyote thistle
of the grasslands rise alert and still
to listen, as if listening were a place
with boundaries each created.

And when we tell our stories,
can they follow the plots, never having seen
the spreading revelation, word by word,
of the wood lily, or the unfolding
revelation of a fruit bat's skin wings?
Can they recognize resolution,
never having watched the constellations
completing their circles around Polaris,
never having studied the rising
and sinking vortexes of a sharp-shinned
hawk circling above a gorge?

Be sure to remember the surprise
among the ashy leaves, that ashy flick
of five-lined skink, living slizard,
and the surprise of burnished mushrooms
sprouting in a ring through black forest
trash. Take notes on the spotted cleaning
shrimp at work with its silver wands
on the mouth of a great reef fish. Assimilate
each polished prick and sun-sharpened claw
of the jumping cholla and learn now
to imitate the bask of the seal,
the sleight of willows in a storm,
to recite the rigid blue illumination
of ice shelves under pressure.

We'll need all these, everything, when we return
to that place after death to tell them, back
to the silent, uniform darknesses we were
before being born on earth.

## If Dying Means Becoming Pure Spirit

Then I think it must be like falling,
that giving-up of the body.
Who wouldn't try to catch hold
of something fast, jerk forward, reaching
with the fingers spread, before the hands
were gone, before the arms
disappeared?

I could never willingly withdraw
from my ribs, pull out of the good bars
and cage, leave the marrow, the temple
of salt, of welling and subsiding, abandon
complacently the swallow, the tongue, the voice.

How could I regard a crab apple
flustered with long-stalked blossoms
or a sycamore hung with nutlets and tufts,
with no face to catch the shadow-splatter
of their limbs and leaves? How could I apprehend
mixed fields of cordgrasses and barleys,
with no breath to detect the scent
of their sedges and clefts?

Even though it's said the spirit
is weightless, still, I think it must be
like falling a terrible fall,
to leave the body, to speed away
backwards, cut off from the humming
*a cappella* of pines, the skeltered
burring of grasshoppers, from the fragrances
of low wood fires beside a river, clean
ice on stalks of cattail and rye, lost
to the purple spice of scattered
thunders, no belly left to feel

the wide, easy range of the earth.

I admit to being angry
and frightened tonight at the thought
of such a plummeting.

## The Laying-on of Hands

There's a gentleness we haven't learned yet,
but we've seen it—the way an early morning haze
can settle in the wayside hedges of lilac and yew,
permeate the emptiness between every scaly
bud and leafstalk until it becomes bound,
fully contained, shaped by the spires,
the stiff pins and purple-white blossoms
of that tangled wall.

There's a subtlety we haven't mastered yet,
but we recognize it—the way moonlight passes
simultaneously upon, through, beyond
the open wing of the crane fly
without altering a single detail
of its smallest paper vein. We know
there is a perfect consideration
of touching possible. The merest snow
accomplishes that, assuming the exact
configuration of the bristled beggarweed
while the beggarweed remains
exclusively itself.

If I could discover that same tension
of muscle myself, if I could move, imagining
smoke finding the forest-lines of the sun
at dusk, if I could place my hand
with that motion, achieve the proper
stance of union and isolation
in fingers and palm, place my hand
with less pressure than a water strider
places by the seeds of its toes
on the surface of the pond, balance
that way, skin to bark, my hand
fully open on the trunk of this elm tree

right now, I know it would be possible
to feel immediately every tissue imposition
and ringed liturgy, every bloodvein
and vacuum of that tree's presence, perceive
immediately both the hard, jerking start
of the seedling in winter and the spore-filled
moss and liquid decay of the fallen trunk
to come, both the angle of tilt in the green sun
off every leaf above and the slow lightning
of hair roots in their buried dark below,
know even the reverse silhouette of my own hand
experienced from inner bark out,
even the moment of this very revelation
of *woman and tree* itself where it was locked
millennia before in those tight molecules
of suckers and sapwood.

Without harm or alteration or surrender
of any kind, I know my hand laid properly,
could discover this much.

## Eating Death

Suppose I had never distinguished myself
to myself from the landscape
so that reaching out to touch a leaf
of chickasaw plum or a spiny pondweed
underwater were no different to me
from putting my hand on my knee or pulling
my fingers through my hair.

And that which was not tangible
I understood as my expression to myself
of my inclinations—my violet serenity
synonomous with distant levels of blue
rain against a ruddy hill, my opening circling
into sex identical with the gold and russet
revolution of the sun into dusk.

In the new forming of lilac
or pear blossoms I realized the color
and fragrance of my balance redefined
every spring. I knew the horizon
as that seam made by the meeting
of my sight and my word, and recognized
the night and the day as my own slow
breathing in and slow breathing out
of light.

Then surely the small ebony hobble
I'd notice one evening appearing
out of an ancient canyon syntax, I'd understand
simply as a further aspect of myself.
And as it became larger, slowly obliterating
the purpose and combustible prairie-presence
of myself, I wouldn't be frightened, knowing
that it came to me from my own depths,

its empty eyes my creation, its steady
grin the white stone of my history.
And when it lifted and spread
its cloak finally, as if it were my will
filling the sky, and I called it my name,
it would be easy to be taken and covered
by my own possession, to put my mouth
against it, my star-pocked arms tight
around its neck, to draw in, sucking,
swallowing, consuming completely
every quiet fold and release
of the last event of my life.

## Berry Renaissance

### I

Its range is worldwide—swamps, pine
and rocky barrens, thickets, dry uplands,
sphagnum-dominated bogs, backyard
gardens—and its names inclusive—cranberry,
nannyberry, strawberry (wood, Indian,
meadow and beach), chokeberry, poison
baneberry, dewberry, dahoon.

### 2

And these are true in certain circles:
at night, a sky-full field of ripe, white
berries; berries of rain that break
on the face; berries, mistletoe and blue,
transformed to pearls and sapphires worn
on eartips and wrists; rose-colored
berries, one at the tip of each breast,
that men like to nibble.

### 3

Of clustered spears and heart-shaped
leaves, of terra-cotta-tinted, lavender
blossoms, of aromatic ovaries, bristled
anthers and stamens, of probings and fiddlings
deep within, of open-eyed sun staring,
of vigil, of transfiguration, of such
is the palate of raspberry liqueur,
blackberry cordial.

# 4

Jumpers in bandana midriffs and short,
handkerchief skirts that fly up to their waists,
jumping fast on their toes, one foot,
both feet, running in, running out, sing
this double, jump-rope chant:

Bearberry, wolfberry,
huckleberry, grape,
partridgeberry, coralberry,
sea and mountainscape—
how many berry-boys did she pick?
one two three four . . .

# 5

*Gospel and the Circle of Redemption*

There are times when I want to be stained,
marked all over by berry wine, baptized,
mouth, fingers, chin and neck, between my toes,
up my legs like the wine-makers of Jerez
who walk round and round in tubs
of berries all day, who return then
to their homes at night wreathed
in berry halos, heady with ripe flower
bouquets dizzy with bees, their bodies
painted, perfumed by purple sun syrup,
their breath elderberry delicious. In the dark
all night, even their sleep is guarded,
lullabied by berry ghosts.

I want to be so immersed, so earth-wined myself

that I'm mistaken for a berry entire.
I want to be plucked, split and gulped whole
by a bacchanal god, swallowed alive by a drunken
savior. I want to rise then from his soul
as his own wild laughter spreading
over the landscape like a berry-colored
evening engulfing blackbirds and cowbirds
and hillside forests and even
every blessing of his own vineyards
and even the way he reclines there,
lordly, generous.

# Apple Disciples

It has always very adequately maintained
its dependents: spider mites, woolly aphids,
brown-tailed moths and flat-headed
borers, canker worms, webworms, green fruit
worms and the red-banded leaf rollers,
all.

It supports, as well, powdery mildew, black rot,
rust, apple scab, apple canker and the hearty
crown gall.

In the field, in the orchard, domesticated,
wild, even at this moment, it endures mincing
mother mice and rutting mice, the needle nips
of jumping mice and dusky-footed wood rats
of temperate zones, also jack rabbits sawing,
mule deer and fallow deer scraping, crunching.

Its tendernesses have been encircled
by the black, biting nails of the apple-eating
porcupine, those sweet dimpled swellings
gnawed clear through to their cores and beyond.
(The stickery pigs waddle off to their burrows
afterward satisfied and full.)

This rosaceas, in its fragrance and sugary
tang, even has the power to draw fearsome
black bears, cinnamon bears all the way down
from their mountain dens to munch and bask
in its frosty shade.

For its pristine example, we also pamper it,
prune it, peel its various parts alive, chop it,
grind it, beat and burn it, crush its droppings

under iron-rimmed wagon wheels, smash
its rotten balls against Old Man Troutman's
barn, get drunk on its golden urine, screech,
bellow, sing of fornicating, fornicate
under its blossomed branches.

Even god, remember, learned early
how best to use such perfect fruit.

## Still Life Abroad

### I

Over the split cantaloupe, its staid,
orderly seeds and corky hide, over
the pall of four plums and the paralysis
of their shriveled leaves, past the still,
steely fish, white stone cheese, biscuits
and bread . . . the little brown hairy hand
moves quickly, brushes the pitcher
of cream, rattles the basket of clams,
suddenly snatches two cherries
from the heap on the plate, jerks back,
disappears. Off-frame, rushing feet,
hysterical chittering can be heard
receding down the invisible hallway.

### II

Within the red serenity of each apple
in the bowl, a seething fortune of molecules
is expanding, uniting, transfiguring.
And at the epicenter of the onion's circle
of steady waves, even in that dark funnel,
there is a hard rush, a gathering
and differentiation of cells rudely forcing
upward toward light a sharp flume of green.
Beneath the quiet surface skin of the bulging
plum, many million microscopic teeth tear,
rip—pulp, fermentation. Tangled in the noiseless
core of one fragrant peach, twist and rear
many fearsome beasts, many fires.

# III

Mary is offering the Baby Jesus an apple.
At least it looks like an apple
from where we stand. But it could easily be
her breast, the blush of the full nipple
cupped in her hand like a pip, held
toward his parted mouth. Or it could be a ripe
bonbon of manna, a heavenly food, or the earth,
juicy, buzzing, spice-popping globe.
It might be the very ovary, the original
blood-and-butter egg of knowledge.
Maybe it's Buddha's ball. Maybe it's Satan's
burning red eye. A jewel, it almost flames,
it almost illuminates.

What should the Mother of God offer
her luscious naked boy-child leaning now
within her arms, against her belly?
And who has the power to forbid any fruit
to the Mother of God and her son?
They make righteousness themselves, moment
by moment. I think it's the apple. Notice
the excitement in his reach, the calm,
rather timid confidence of her inward
gaze. And although no one can be certain
about the future, it seems apparent to us
from the zeal on his baby lips
that he means to accept.

## *Foreplay*

When it first begins, as you might expect,
the lips and thin folds are closed, the pouting
layers pressed, lapped lightly,
almost languidly, against one another
in a sealed bud.

However, with certain prolonged
and random strokings of care
along each binding line, with soft
intrusions traced beneath each pursed
gathering and edge, with inquiring
intensities of gesture—as the sun
swinging slowly from winter back
to spring, touches briefly,
between moments of moon and masking
clouds, certain stunning points
and inner nubs of earth—so
with such ministrations, a slight
swelling, a quiver of reaching,
a tendency toward space,
might be noticed to commence.

Then with dampness from the dark,
with moisture from the falling
night of morning, from hidden places
within the hills, each seal begins
to loosen, each recalcitrant clasp
sinks away into itself, and every tucked
grasp, every silk tack willingly relents,
releases, gives way, proclaims a turning,
declares a revolution, assumes,
in plain sight, a surging position
that offers, an audacious offering
that beseeches, every petal parted wide.

Remember the spiraling, blue
valerian, remember the violet, sucking
larkspur, the laurel and rosebay
and pea cockle flung backwards, remember
the fragrant, funnelling lily, the lifted
honeysuckle, the sweet, open pucker
of the ground ivy blossom?

Now even the darkest crease possessed,
the most guarded, pulsing, least drop
of pearl bead, moon grain trembling
deep within is fully revealed, fully exposed
to any penetrating wind or shaking fur
or mad hunger or searing, plunging surprise
the wild descending sky in delirium
has to offer.

# The Power of Sun

## I

I think those who have its name
are luckiest—most fortunate sun bear,
sun grebe and sun bittern, sunflower,
sun spider, sunfish, sunbeam snake.

And the name is apt, for the sun bear
rises, reveals his orange-crested chest,
flares with huffings and hot, bellowing
pronouncements over the quiet of damp
liverworts, mosses and mangroves,
just like the morning.

The amethyst, green-headed sun
bird sucks and shimmers his wings,
perching on yellow petals and beams
of buds, like summer sun. And the sunstone
glows as reddish as a spangled dusk,
and the sun spider is golden and swift,
like a tight circle of sun focused
through a glass, spiking its way
across the grasses. Sunfish—rock bass,
bluegill and pumpkinseed—are buoyed
all over with flashing spines and shafts.
They float and yawn light through
and through underwater.

Maybe the name comes first, the word
a binding predestination fulfilled
only subsequently with a proper being,
as a sea wind wild and whipping
against a fractured cliff comes first
and then the cypress emerges, gnarls

and knobs itself to fit the shape
of that buffeting.

Think how the sun starfish can press
its limy rays outward, striving
to fill the possibilities of sweeping
combustion in its infinite name
all of its life.

And back, back inside that first final
locus of black beginning void, I believe
the sound of *sun* must suddenly
have been sung, and then, of course,
it had to happen.


## 2


Someone said my real name to me
last night. Someone whispered
to me, before I knew, the name he knew
me to become last night.

*Sun breath* he murmured into my mouth;
*sun hands sun-caressing* he said,
kissing the ends of my fingers;
he called me *sun voice low and catching
through parting forest rain; ruddy
sun beaded nipples* drawn and bitten
by his lips; *sun thighs* he whispered,
tasting with his tongue, *rocking slow
with salt on the sea; light as solar wind,
self-luminous body* he called me again
and again. And I rose easily to my name
as if over the rim of the earth at dawn,
exhumed and spacious, shining

in his arms, as boundless and blinding
and released in that given radiance
as death by its name could never hope
to be in all of its dark freedom.

## Are Some Sins Hosannas?

Those sins, for example, of amplitude,
of over-abundance, like the unrestrained
seeding of the blue yucca, the mink frog
and dusky crawfish frog, the spore-gorged
tumbling puffball? You've seen this transgression
in the cottonwood too, covering the river,
burdening the summer with more drifting,
white fluff and flurry than anyone
ever requested, replicating over and over
and over, as if being were worth it.

Are certain sins, of arrogance for instance,
a form of praise, the way the mullein
and the vinegar weed shoot straight up
from the earth unabashed, taking
overmuch pride in their stances, pointing
their flower-covered batons toward the sky
as if they were a righteousness?
This is the same haughty act the stalks
of sotol and steeplebush, the audacious
lodgepole pine and towering lousewort perform.

Is the noise of too much joy a madness
condemned by more moderate gods
who surely know better? Hush, hush
chortling heathen toads, unredeemed, triple-
chirping field crickets, ceaseless
sinning *tsee* of waxwings, spring-forest
*sweet-sweet-sweet* of wood warblers.

If some sins are truly jubilations,
then with you here beside me again
tonight, I'm certain I offend
many gods myself. I confess it and repent,

repent with the most contrite
voice I can manage, pulling my pillow
over my face, lying on my hands to try
to stop this rude sacrilege, my uncontrollable
crooning of happiness, incessant caressing,
touching your body everywhere, a sliding
vine of butterfly pea openly curling,
binding, such decadent opulence, my long,
excessive murmurs of immeasurable
adoration.

## This Kind of Grace

Let's bless the body before love.
By rights we should, every detail.
We could use water, spring water
or rose, minted or bay rum. A touch
to the shoulders—*bless these.* A drop
behind each knee—*sanctify here.* A sprinkle
to the belly, yours, mine—*in heartfelt*
*appreciation.*

I could dip my fingers into oil cupped
in my palm, sweet citronella, lavender,
clove, trace your forehead, temple
to temple, the boldness of that warm
stone—*so glorified*—perfume the entire
declaration of your spine, neck
to tail—*so hallowed.*

We'd neglect nothing, ankle, knuckle,
thigh, cheek. And for the rapture
of hair, scented with sweat or the spices
of cedary sages and summer pines,
in which I hide my face—*praise*
*to the conjoining hosts of all*
*radiant forests and plains.*

And imagine how I'd lay my hand,
move my hand carefully on and around
and under each axil and hummock and whorl
between your legs, the magnificent maze
of those gifts—*thanks to the exploding*
*heavens, thanks to all pulsing suns.*

For these cosmic accomplishments:
this delve of your body, a narrow

crevasse leading into earth-darkness;
this assertion of your hands, light
winds lifting, parting, pressing
upon supine grasses; this rise, the tip
of a swollen moon over black hills;
this sweep of union, hawk-shadow
falling fast across the open prairie
into the horizon; *for this whole blessed*
*body, for what we are about to receive*
*together tonight . . . truly, ardently,*
*ecstatically, boundlessly*
*grateful.*

## Fetal Bat: The Creation of the Void

Tender in its absolute predestination—four
long, deformed finger bones, plum-round
body, umbrella wings—it's an inevitability
begun by bat penis, sperm dart, bat
ovum, bat pocket of womb where it flutters,
flickers sporadically, warm and drowned
in swaying pearl-clear waters.

The fetus folds in its place, tightens,
settles again, shoulder-hunched knuckles
drawn to its ears, a vestigial claw
to its chin. Its eyes are thinly lidded.
Its tongue, slender, pliable as a single
leaflet of summer fern, moves back
slightly in its throat as if to suckle.

A pea-sized heart swings inside
the tiny night of its chest inside the night
behind its mother's teats and blue
coming-milk inside the still stone cavern
of night where she hangs by one foot upside
down inside the universe of night
with its shifting, combusting summary
of stars wheeling inside, outside.

When this fetus emerges,
feet first, born alive, clinging
to its mother's breast, legs curled
beneath her arm pit, drying the fine fuzz
of its face and features, the translucent
dun and veined-scarlet silk skin
of its wings stretched wide, it screams,
screeches wildly, setting every petal
of yucca and sweet chicory that blooms

inside its rare garden to shivering,
to ringing.

What a very first phenomenon
it makes as it occupies so perfectly
such a definite empty space, the only void
of itself which we recognize now
never anywhere, until this moment
of its birth, existed at all.

## *Infanticide*

Sometimes they were put in baskets, little nests
of rushes and leaves. (Someone had to weave
these water-cradles for them—the threading
fingers of grandmother, auntie, midwife.)
They were placed in their casket-boats
and launched, and if they couldn't swim,
whose fault was that?

Some were curled, heads touching knees,
in their womb positions inside clay jars,
then set along temple porticoes
in case some passing worshipper might want
a baby for a slave. Their fretting
voices in the corridors were as common
and hoarse as dry cicadas, till they died.

Some were burned for expiation to the gods,
in ceremonies, shrill trumpets and cymbals
covering their cries. Some were placed naked,
still bloody, on icy pinnacles in dark snow.
Some were strangled, some tortured
to death, some eaten, a few hours old.
After all, nobody knew them yet.

Some were flung off canyon cliffs,
even on a spring afternoon, the prairie
colored with clover and milkvetch,
or even on a damp autumn morning,
the plums red and sweet and fragrant.

Mary Hamilton bore her baby alone
in the King's forest, leaning back, pressing
against an oak, her skirts pulled up,
and all the while watching the patterns

above her, layered leaves, sky pieces,
branches and boughs constricting, widening
with the wind. Then she killed it with a knife.

Gone, murdered by deliberate
acts—I don't think anyone
ever counted them all—those cursed, born
during lightning storms or under a bad
moon or feetfirst or blind, born
during war or a hard journey, into starvation,
those with the wrong fathers, the girls,
the unwanted. It was the custom,
and there were reasons, burdens.
Even mothers said so.

From every stone-cut or gnawed
umbilical, from every bud-sized
fist, every thumb and finger petal
folded inward, from every perfectly
stitched violet thread, every temple pulse,
every rib shudder of this elegy,
relieve us.

# Goddamn Theology

It was easier when you were a jonquil
and I was a fingertip pressed at the juncture
of your radiating petals and stiff stem.
And it was not so difficult
when I was a Persian guitar
and you were the knee on which I lay,
my neck held easily in your hand.

But there were problems
when you were two hundred years of years,
twisted like taffy, twisted and looped
like a dry bristlecone in dusty snow,
and I was just a beginning sliver
of clear, tadpole breath in a whorl
of waterweed. I didn't know
what to say.

And when I thought I knew your name,
and I called it out loud many times,
that's when you were a deaf sheaf
of catacombed coral with more
than one title and no tongue.

I was whole, a burning ball of peach
hanging from a branch. You were multiple,
sparks struck from a hammer against rock.
I split into a showering orbit of mayflies
in the evening sun. You congealed
into a seeded cow patty in the field.

When the painted pony and I were galloping
fast through rabid waves on the beach,
there you were, a tiny spire of ship
sailing off the edge of the sea.

The night I woke in white, my body moon-grey,
you were curled, a black hump of quilt
at the foot of my bed, dead asleep.

And later when you were falling rapidly,
heavily, raindrops and pockdrops and bullet
marks, a mob in the mountain lake, I was precise
wing and talon over the prairie, jack-knifing
and stabbing, lifting the mouse by her spine.

When I was crying, crying and truly
sorry, you were a spray of chartreuse
and scarlet tinfoil confetti on my head.

That's when I knew for certain
it was going to be much more difficult
than we'd ever imagined before.

# The Natural Nature of Late Night Prayers

Most are generally horribly tangled,
like the broken-twig broom of a witch hazel
or the sticky, irregular web of a branchtip
spider, like the leaf-jumble of a squirrel's
nest empty since last season or the stumble,
the bandy-legged hops of a drunk man
down a curb, the zip-zag dance of fire
up a dry pine. Like thistles and fur, late
night prayers are usually snarled, embrangled.

The ones I know are always more knotted
than smooth, like long hair wet with salt
and whipping in an ocean wind, like long hair
stroked and gripped and left against a pillow
after love, always crumpled like hoarded
riffraff (limp seaweed, crab bones, jelly
strings, seadollar teeth, plastic kelp)
wave-wadded on a shore. Prayers accumulate
rubble in the dark like rat hovels.

To be unresolvable must be the ordained
nature of after-midnight prayers; for never
neat, never orderly, never sorted, never
clear-headed, never singularly purposeful,
always shaken with knocks, overburdened
with rattles, bound with ear-numbing
babbles, my own, crooked mottles, stutters,
sheet-wringings and whines, now again
beside the bedpost my rambling accusations,
now again my mad apologies.

# Trial and Error

The right prayer might be a falling
prayer spiralling down in the throats
and raised wings and white warmth
of tumbling pigeons, the joy
of a beseeching abandon, or a crossing
prayer in the fingers of oak branches
over themselves, their display
of a hopeful wind, or a drifting
prayer in the cerise petals
loosed and dropping from a stalk
of wild betony, a proclamation
in dissolution.

It may take two every night, maybe three
every dawn—prayers offered of one fact
against another—milkweed against winter,
reflected face against water, rapid
barking against fear.

I can compose any kind, prayers wrapped
in seaweed, rolled in grape leaves,
prayers sent spinning tied to butterfly
kites crackling in the sky over the sea,
prayers in wax bound to stones sunk
past coral cliffs or ice canyons
to the ocean floor, prayers delivered
with moans or howls, rattling gourds
or timbals, prayers in the cadence of rain,
prayers in the absence of breath.

I'll send them out in signs, lanterns
on rooftops, candles on cairns, backward
prayers like the dark side of the moon, prayers
hung upside down by the knees, prayers

beginning with praise, beginning with *Our Father,*
with *Darling Mother,* with *Darkling Son,* fading
off fast to *In the beginning* . . .

I'll become by myself, I swear,
whatever prayer it takes, teeth, eyelids,
ears, beatitude of knuckles, invocation
of spine, a solid skeleton of the perfectly
linked linguistics of prayer, hands
pressed together before me,
my whole body speaking,
waiting.

## God Alone

It was important on this April night
to open the windows, all of them, east
and on the west, pushing the panes
as high as they would go, to allow
the wind free passage through the rooms,
to allow the night occupancy
as if it were a word come into the body
to render the bones definitive.

And the house became the spring
night—the hallway a vernal hallway
rushed with flowing field grasses, all
the tugs and crescents of sex-in-flight.
The wooden casements, railings and rungs,
were carved, their curves traced,
by the calls of peepers, crickets,
killdeer, those cries possessing
every mirror too, in and out, like streaks
and bells of light. Quilts and counterpanes
became shadowed with yellow-budded willow
and lilac priorities, like patterns
laid out, wound and stitched fast.
In the dark, a garden of grape,
honeysuckle and rosmarin took root,
spreading, blooming, vining a leafy
network through the bedroom mid-air.

And the April night, rich with black
stellar vacancies and portents, became
the house, took the grace of pliant
curtains lifting and parting, took
the form of doorways, cornices,
ceilings, pressed to the frame of every
room angle, curled inside the painted

rings and links of porcelain curios
on the shelves, settled in the open
drawers of the bureau, the hollowness
beneath the bed, became fluted
with the fanned linen of the lampshade,
rigid with the wooden chair, spindled
with beveled legs and back. Shaping
itself to faces and fingers, the night
became human. It gave and received
the same breath with all who slept there.

Divine is the spring night filling
the house with fragrant tumbling,
with the cylindrical sounds and high-climbing
purposes of a sun-tilted earth; and equally divine
are the rooms providing the boundless black
with measurement, with place, with the reflections
and honor of artifact; and equally divine
is the hand that raised all the sashes.

## Another Little God

You don't know how important
it might be—the blue-white light
from a star like Vega caught in the eyedots
of nocturnal grass frogs and yellow-bellied
toads, caught in the senses of fishing
bats, mouse-tailed bats.

And I can't say either how much
it might matter—that same ping
of light multiplied by each reflective
grain of crystal sand along a beach
beside the Gulf, held by each slide
and scissor of beak rushes
in a southern marsh.

Maybe particles and spears of light
from Vega penetrate the earth, descend
through silt and loam, touching,
even enlivening, even partially defining
the microscopic roots of bellflowers,
purple vetches and peas, the creases
and shackles of worm snakes and grubs.

The translucent eggs of the plumed moth,
the fins of the redbelly dace might need
a star's blue-white light, like water,
like air. Breath might require it,
breathing starlight into the heart.
You don't know. After all, we've never
lived without it.

If starlight spears through each oily
sperm link of reedbuck and potto,
if it enters every least bulb

of snow flea, wheel bug, hay
louse, if it corridors through all bone
crystals, around each spurl and bole
of the brain, inside timbre and voice,
piercing the whole stone and space
of *believe*, then, if only for one
complete name under the sky tonight,
lie still and remember.

## Life in an Expanding Universe

It's not only all those cosmic
pinwheels with their charging solar
luminosities, the way they spin around
like the paper kind tacked to a tree trunk,
the way they expel matter and light
like fields of dandelions throwing off
waves of summer sparks in the wind,
the way they speed outward,
receding, creating new distances
simply by soaring into them.

But it's also how the noisy
crow enlarges the territory
above the landscape at dawn, making
new multiple canyon spires in the sky
by the sharp towers and ledges
of its calling; and how the bighorn
expand the alpine meadows by repeating
inside their watching eyes every foil
of columbine and bell rue, all
the stretches of sedges, the candescences
of jagged slopes and crevices existing there.

And though there isn't a method
to measure it yet, by finding
a golden-banded skipper on a buttonbush,
by seeing a blue whiptail streak
through desert scrub, by looking up
one night and imagining the fleeing
motions of the stars themselves, I know
my presence must swell one flutter-width
wider, accelerate one lizard-slip farther,
descend many stellar-fathoms deeper
than it ever was before.

## Creating Transfiguration

It only took staying still, standing
in the right place at the right time, arms
held out sideways straight from the body,
standing still like that on the shore, the winter
wind blowing ice-fog and freezing spray
in from the sea in swelling shrouds
and moanings all night;

to stand there, ice slowly shelling
the body in smooth white glass,
forming, hour by hour, thick glistening
pillars around bone, frost tassels
of tangled hair, clear, solid ribbons
of sea frozen in fringe hanging down
from the fingers and chin, furrowing
like tears stopped on the cheeks;

only to stand still letting the stinging
sea-drizzle fasten to face and breast
in the dark, form choirs of ice on spine,
ribs, knuckles, name; to stay at dawn,
staring unmoved toward the horizon, crystal
body gold in the sun, steam rising
like a holy spirit of light in the sun;

then to let them all, waking, come,
some running, some on knees, some bringing
candles in paper cups, peaches dried
with clove, some carrying violet lilies
and spindled whelks, others placing markers,
smooth stones, like loaves of bread, piled
in cairns on the sand for signs, all
circling round and round, all imbued
and radiant, all promising,
all transfigured.

## The Fancy of Free Will

All of us here were taught
that we were born believing
in the beauty of the deliberately twisted,
the supervised tangle, the cultivated
knot. So we adore any loveliness
that turns in on itself, compounding
the strength of its simple charms—the bud-stitched
apple inverted four times, the five-knuckled
thumb, the bisected line melded
to its opposite ligament.

We know that no two crafted knurls,
knitted creatures or finely gnarled
blossoms can ever be exactly the same,
this uniqueness thus proving
their worth and superiority.

And how could anything growing
without the guidance of shaping straps
and stakes and restricting wires
ever hope to become the beauty
beyond itself?

The artist of my body wore
black satin lounging pajamas
every time she came. She carried
into my room her satchels filled
with splints, adjustable buckles, tight
nylon sheaths, choking thongs and staves,
metal strips, measuring rods in many sizes,
all enchanting, magical materials
which she fitted in ingenious ways
to the raw material of my limbs
and torso. If there was pain,

I thought of the wondrous perfume
she wore—the third generation of mulled
and humped gardenia gourd.

Unless told to turn, to widen,
to squeeze, I lay still
as she worked, tying, splitting,
sometimes separating, sometimes
inserting, binding and directing my bones
and flesh, always consulting her design.
She was a saint in her concentration
and mastery.

Now tonight, if you doubt
we're right, just watch the adoration,
the rapture on this boy's face
as he unwinds the binding cords
from my refined feet, as he removes
the tight swaddling cloths around one thigh,
the metal braids banding the other. He kisses
each warm convolution he discovers,
each devised angle, caresses with his fingers
the surprising crevice, the damp
revelation. His lips and tongue
are around each epiphany
as he uncovers it, learning a new
language, slowly, eagerly, flushed.
See his hands tremble with pleasure.
He's exalted, a witness to god momentarily,
as he anticipates the hidden art beyond,
unhooking, unbelting, easing away
the final brace, lifting carefully
the last silk shift.

## For Any Known Fact: Nude Walking
### Alone on a Beach in Moonlight

One might easily become confused
about proper designations. The beach
is as white, as tense and dedicated
as the moon, it could be stated.
Or should one say the moon presses
through the black sky as steady, reflective
and waxen as a nude body sequined
with spray walks through the night?

The sound of such convoluted thinking
has the same sound as the surf, perhaps;
for the speaking surf has many tongues
that divulge and stutter, prod forward
fondling, withdrawing.

The black sea surface glitters
with bobbing, stuttering moons as flat
as light. Likewise the black body
of any single fish is covered
with thousands of glassy moons, and each drop
of spray on a nude body—jewelling the neck,
beading the lashes, tresses and ear tips,
sparkling down the ivory legs—becomes moon
and mirror simultaneously.

Along the beach of the one distant,
completely naked moon, a strolling figure
might be detected. The moon is a mirror,
surely, but is a mirror a forbidden window
becoming itself by its own reflective act,
or is it just a dull word of unenlightened
imitation?

To turn and walk deliberately out
into the convoluted surf, to feel
the dedicated sounds of that surf
rising gradually to cover the thighs,
the breasts, the eyes, to say the sinking
lungs are filled with waves of fondling
moons, the heart stopped with silent
salt-light—it could be called *suicide*,
but that's just a single word, a thrashing
sound covered with reflective scales,
a stuttering word that might mean to see
suddenly, in this black and alabaster
world, a orange-violet reflection
in a transfigured window, a startling
scarlet-blue sphere of body
and image as one, or it might mean
merely to watch, without interfering,
as that barely recognizable figure
of white light unclothed in the mirror
steps precisely and manifestly off
the edge of the moon.

## The Image in a World of Flux

As black as tropic heat on a windowless
night, black as the center of poison, black
as the scorched edges of an old prayer, the cat
sits upright, tail curled around her paws.

She's the only consistent being here
for as far as anyone can see, surrounded
as she is by shooting and sinking pellets
of plains, by fields that startle in rattles
and coughs, rivers that mend in curtsies,
relinquish in spells, reclaim
in gales and graveyards.

Yet she sits, a composition of bone
and bevy, throat strumming, satiated,
oriental, dozing. Her reflection on the sky
in the swarmy sea is split open and sealed
constantly, copped and bound, snatched
in hooks of salt, rocked by pistons
and wheels of water, fang and whisker
drawn under, yawning and licking lifted up.

Her reflection rests serene in puzzled
fragments on the glass dome smashed
and glued together again and again.

As still as a marble saint in a vault,
as stopped as *12:00 midnight* spoken aloud,
she's the measuring rod, the magnetic pole,
the spine, the axis around which the rackets
of the surf strike, ameliorate, reverse
themselves, define their exploding equations,
deny their names in fog and ice. She's the base
tagged and abandoned repeatedly.

Watch out. Watch out. There's a sudden
conflagration. A flame catches hold
at the corner of this picture beginning
to crisp and curl under, smoke and ashes moving
rapidly in a diagonal across the world
toward my fingers.

But see, she's leaping, leaping,
white now, invisible, up and out, escaping
to clutch a bare branch as real and definite
as this network of black cracks we see spread
in its steady place across the blank,
blank ceiling over our heads.

# The All-Encompassing
### Philosopher in Meditation,
### by Rembrandt

The philosopher is the old, bearded
man in the red beanie, dozing,
it seems, in the sun by the window.
Before him on the table lies his ponderous
volume open to the indirect
light of the day.

But the philosopher could be
the bent firekeeper by the wall
behind the stairs. He stirs, rouses
the coals, studies the combustion.
He's hunched and crotchety there,
concentrating obviously as he constructs
his viable conflagration.

The solid spiral, helix staircase,
curving down the middle of the room,
could be the philosophy, each step leading
naturally and logically to the next.
It's the physical form of ordered thought
reaching a grand staircase conclusion.
The carpenter, then, is the missing seer.

Yet the small round door (dwarf-size)
behind the old man, rightly accepts,
by portal philosophy, that it must meditate
on its closed and locked condition
until a key appears, at which time
it must assimilate the revelation of *open*.

Does the blind black in the corners
beyond the reach of the window radiance,

as well as the cavern maw at the top
curve of the stairs, match the oblivion
in the sleep of the thinker? If so,
then the sun works a philosophy itself
by realizing the window ledge, the pottery
on the sill and idle book, the folded hands,
the dropped chin. And the old scholar
sleeps in the light of the known.

O philosopher's meditation, don't you understand,
even the baskets and barrels and pots
and smoke of this hovel that split
and bang and cling, and the firekeeper
cracking his throat and the bucket
of ashes and clinkers on the hearth,
and each separate meditation in its place
and time, all these must take their positions
in the rhetoric of the system?

If I hear the ancient housewife rattling
and creaking now down the curve of the stairs
(old gene, spiral of conception, old twist),
dogs scrambling at her heels, broom
and dustpan knocking, if she enters here
with her raucous retinue, cursing and barking,
jolts the sleeper, sweeping under the old man's
stool, cuffs the firekeeper, sets the pans
and spoons swinging, then all previous
suppositions fail, and we must begin again.

Photo by Yvonne Mozée

Pattiann Rogers has published five books of poetry: *The Expectations of Light* (Princeton, 1981), *The Tattooed Lady in the Garden* (Wesleyan, 1986), *Legendary Performance* (Ion Press, 1987), *Splitting and Binding* (Wesleyan, 1989), and *Geocentric* (Gibbs Smith, 1993). She has been the recipient of two NEA grants, a Guggenheim Fellowship, and a Lannan Poetry Fellowship. Her poems have won several prizes, including the Tietjens Prize and the Hokin Prize from *Poetry*, the Roethke Prize from *Poetry Northwest*, the Strousse Award from *Prairie Schooner*, two book awards from the Texas Institute of Letters, and four Pushcart Prizes. She is a graduate of the University of Missouri (B.A.) and the University of Houston (M.A.) and has been a visiting writer at the University of Texas, the University of Montana, and the University of Arkansas and a member of the faculty of Vermont College. The mother of two grown sons, Pattiann Rogers lives with her husband, a geophysicist, in Colorado.

## MORE CONTEMPORARY POETRY FROM MILKWEED EDITIONS:

**Civil Blood**
Jill Breckenridge

**The Color of Mesabi Bones**
John Caddy

**The Phoenix Gone, The Terrace Empty**
Marilyn Chin

**Astonishing World**
**Selected Poems of Ángel González 1956-1986**
Translated from the Spanish
by Steven Ford Brown

**One Age in a Dream**
Diane Glancy

**Paul Bunyan's Bearskin**
Patricia Goedicke

**The Tongues We Speak**
Patricia Goedicke

**Boxelder Bug Variations**
Bill Holm

**The Dead Get By with Everything**
Bill Holm

**The Freedom of History**
Jim Moore

**The House in the Sand**
Pablo Neruda
Translated from the Spanish
by Dennis Maloney and Clark Zlotchew